MATERIAL CHANGE

"Our Forefathers"

In our hands they deposited
The tools to interweave our dreams,
What we see, what we feel, what we live.

In the weaving they taught us how
To weave with yarn from the rainbow,
Colors, with the fragrance of our country,
From this, we cultivate and harvest.

They, too, did it this way, like this they flowered,
Today we, their children, mark new trails,
Together with our greatest teachers.

– Fausto Contreras Lazo

MATERIAL CHANGE

Design Thinking and
the Social Entrepreneurship
Movement

Eve Blossom
Foreword by Yves Behar
New photography by Mark Standen
Metropolis Books

CONTENTS

FOREWORD
Yves Behar

The best design work—and the design work with the greatest longevity—is formed through partnerships, not short-term engagements. Think of George Nelson's and Charles and Ray Eameses' work with Herman Miller, or Richard Sapper's with IBM. What interests me in design is building a foundation and a legacy that will last well after the designer is no longer there. Create those and you are cultivating enduring values that are integral to the way a company works. To influence how brands respond to and fit within important issues in the world, designers and their clients need to collaborate.

We are now extending the idea of partnership outward, to include not only the designer and the producer but the customer as well. It used to be, in design, that most things you wanted to know about the customer came from the marketing team. But now the Internet and social media allow for direct dialogue among designers, producers, and customers. Together, we can have conversations about what buyers think, what they believe, and what they want to stand behind. It's not simply about "voting with your money," as was done in the past. It's a new way of supporting companies by actually engaging with them. This means an improved relationship between the designer, the producer, and the consumer, and it also affords a better way to deliver a product.

Buyers have become disenchanted with the form of consumption where everybody buys the same thing. Too often, they feel disconnected from the things they own. Compare this to the times when craft and objects were a lot more individualized: people felt closer to the goods they owned. Today, consumers expect much more from their brands: they want to participate in the creation of the products themselves. Ultimately, it's about being part of a new form of customized buying through dialogue and participation.

I believe all of this indicates that we are moving from the age of mass production into the age of mass individualization. Designers who bring values to their work—be they social, ecological, or other—make products that are desirable by connecting with people. This is the way to build brand loyalty today. In fact, this form of participation may be the new brand loyalty.

Sustainability and notions of social good are the new values of the twenty-first century, and designers need to integrate them into every project they do, every relationship with industry that they have. We have a huge role to play in ensuring that these values are seen as assets; they must help create a product that is incredibly attractive, delightful, exciting, and commercially viable.

But it is also critical that the local culture—that is, the people who make the materials or the products—be partners in the ownership of the projects. This level of ownership has three very important effects: it integrates the product or service into its context; it allows the product or service to function on its own merits; and it *always* brings a lot more solutions to the table.

Lulan Artisans builds on this practice of local ownership by allowing design to flourish rather than remain stuck in a cultural cliché. Founder Eve Blossom has built her company around the participation of true partners, and the dialogue that ensues—about designing and making—is central to its philosophy, its success, and its usefulness as a blueprint for others to follow. This approach enables artisans not just to keep their traditional crafts alive but to help them thrive. It also aligns goals and generates social good. Lulan is a new model for an exchange of service that goes far beyond a purely economic exchange.

What does the future of design look like? It looks like this.

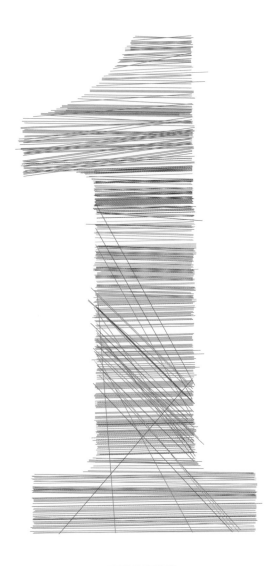

**THE POWER
OF CIRCUMSTANCE**

A PATTERN IN THE THREADS

It was 1992, in a marketplace in Hanoi, North Vietnam. Chickens wandered about, clucking madly. Vendors sold everything from flowers and vegetables to toys and jewelry. Fish swirled in barrels, freshly pulled from the nearby Mekong River. Myriad chockablock stalls displayed herbs and spices. The aromas of mint, cilantro, turmeric, pepper, and ginger mixed headily in the air.

The waves of tourists who would later flood Cambodia, Laos, and Vietnam had not yet arrived. The United States still limited its commerce with Vietnam under a lingering provision of the Trading with the Enemy Act that wasn't lifted until 1994. The few travelers were mostly from Europe, Australia, and other Asian countries. Occasionally, an American ex-serviceman would pass through to visit places from his youthful past, seeking closure from the dust and gunpowder of his wartime experience.

Stepping into the streets of Hanoi was like stepping back in time. Brownouts happened frequently. Intersections had no traffic lights. Air conditioning was a luxury. Most Vietnamese rode bicycles for transport. Traffic was a mix of rickshaws, some motorbikes, and the occasional car. The city also revealed striking contrasts—a boarded-up opera house served mostly as a convenient urinal, while Hoan Kiem Lake, in the center of town,

A POWERFUL MOMENT

There's something going on in design—something powerful. People have realized a simple truth: Design is a legitimate way to change the world. Design can also change the fundamental building blocks of business. From household products to social interactions, people are using design to produce some previously unexpected results.

Why? Because we realize that our purchases have implications beyond the short-term satisfactions of goods we buy. We understand that the plastic bottles we use many times a day to gulp down water, soda, or juice will be around for hundreds of years longer than the few moments during which we hold them in our hands. Although most of us are aware of such issues, we still live with these failures of design, knowing solutions are needed.

An increasing number of people are also concerned with the pesticides and growth enhancers that coat the leaves of our food and get pulled in through the roots. We realize that we are what we eat and go to great lengths to obtain organic, locally grown food. The small back-to-the-earth movement of the 1960s and 1970s has spread internationally. Whole Foods Market, for instance, started with a single small store in Austin, Texas, in 1980. Today, it's a world leader in natural and organic foods, was a serene respite where Vietnamese couples and families strolled with ice cream. I was in the middle of a yearlong journey of personal and professional exploration, after an intense two-year stretch at the respected architecture firm Gensler. Travels in Southeast Asia took me through Cambodia, Laos, Vietnam, Thailand, India, Nepal, Malaysia, and Indonesia via deafening motorbikes, rickety buses, compact trains, and primitive boats. Along the way, I stopped at every open-air marketplace I could find and immediately sought out the textile vendors. As a designer, I was intoxicated by the beauty and craftsmanship of their wares.

Moving deeper into the Hanoi market, I came across a section filled with fabrics, sarongs, and scarves of every color and texture—silky and smooth, or thick with a rough weave. High-quality pieces of silk and cotton had been carefully folded and stacked on small tables. Traditional woven sarongs, some two yards long, in deep purples, indigo blues, and strong reds; ikats, made with tie-dyed yarns; and rich brocades were everywhere. Many featured multicolored, intricate patterns and traditional motifs of birds and diamonds. The market for antique textiles had just started to pick up among French, Japanese, and other Asian travelers, so the oldest, most valuable fabrics were locked away in cases. Intrigued, I wanted to find out where and how these handwoven pieces were made—the process, the designs, and the people doing this amazing work.

//

an $8 billion company with more than 270 stores in North America and the United Kingdom and 54,000 employees. Whole Foods has been a dominant force pushing this new way of living and eating into the mainstream, compelling other major food retailers to offer natural products and showing Wall Street that a health-conscious, eco-friendly company can draw big money. From its business model, to its supply chain, to the stores themselves, Whole Foods proves how indebted its success is to design—a holistic, systemic design that considers every aspect and layer of the business from bottom to top.

In a larger sense, we consumers have redefined ourselves as citizens of the world— or, at least, participants in a global system that needs to reflect our broadened values of civility. Lifestyles of Health and Sustainability, or "LOHAS," buyers—those who base purchasing decisions on socioeconomic factors including a company's commitment to justice and sustainability—are emerging as an economic powerhouse. More than 63 million LOHAS-minded consumers now spend $230 billion each year, according to Conscious Media and Lifestyles of Health and Sustainability. In 2009, customers worldwide spent more than $4 billion on fair trade products alone— a 22 percent increase over the previous year, according to Fairtrade Labelling Organizations International.

I stood transfixed, cradling a piece of fabric in my hands. As my eyes traveled its length, admiring the soft texture and fine craftsmanship, something stirred deep in my soul. The intimate, human scale of the fabric resonated with me. Though I had much to learn about Vietnam's weaving history, I realized that a piece of fabric contains a sense of place, in terms of what it means to a culture, to a people, and to their daily life and rituals. I was hooked.

With translation help and a flurry of hand signals, I discovered from the woman behind the tables, Anh, that the cloth had been made nearby. I learned that there are entire villages in Southeast Asia organized around agriculture and weaving—places like Ha Dong and Sapa, several hours outside of Hanoi, or Tan Chau, farther north, which produces a silk dyed black with the diospyros fruit. Bound by strong traditions, they constructed cloth the same way it had been woven for centuries. I was determined to see these places and meet the artisans who created these masterpieces. "How can I visit them?" I asked. Anh said, cheerfully, "I will take you tomorrow." Her answer would change my life.

The next morning, I took off with Anh on her motorbike to one of the nearby weaving villages. After a short journey, Anh, also my translator, led me around, happily showing

This lifestyle shift touches us in dozens of ways every day. It plays out when we pause in the supermarket aisle to choose among various products; when we sort our refuse into a blue or green recycling bin rather than blindly dump it into a trash can; or even when we discuss investments with our financial advisors.

A fast-growing segment of the population is interested in buying according to its values. Those values differ from person to person and in relation to various product categories, such as soap or cars. Also, these customers want to both understand and trust a manufacturer's or service provider's claims. The reality is that some people have always wanted to buy according to their values, whether in support of "Dolphin Safe," "Conflict Free," or "Organically Grown." It's just easier today to know a product's provenance and to verify a producer's claims. Among the ever varying blend of groups, individuals, markets, and companies, these values are all equally important to address—which makes for an interesting and crucial puzzle for designers to solve.

A new category of buyer is examining the entire product-creation cycle, not only for ecological and social reasons but also to determine how the overall impact of production reflects their values. Customers are focusing, many for the first time, on the earliest stages of a product's inception and execution, with a special eye on the me her world. I saw for the first time a scene of bustling activity that I would experience again and again throughout Southeast Asia on what would become regular trips to the region.

Houses were perched on stilts about 9 feet high to protect them from flooding, and in the sheltered, open-air spaces underneath sat women at wooden looms. A quick glance revealed dozens of weavers, methodically setting the warp or weaving. I heard the clacking of looms as they tightened down the threads. I saw the dyers boiling water, mixing dyes, dipping and rinsing the skeins, and then hanging them to dry in the sun. Their color blends were rich and deep: a range of yellows from canary to mustard made from jackfruit wood, intense browns from the betel palm, and dark blues and blacks from indigo plants.

Historically, women started weaving in Southeast Asia during the off-season, when they were not farming rice. Between yields, they made traditional sarongs for themselves and for extended family. Sarongs are long, tube-shaped pieces of fabric worn by men and women. One steps into the center of the tube, pulls it up to the waist, and folds the excess fabric down to hold it in place. In some areas of Southeast Asia, people still wear sarongs every day, in other areas, sarongs are for special events, such as weddings.

manufacturing process and how products and services are designed. They are considering their purchases in a holistic sense, examining the price of products not only in terms of the amount paid at the register but also in the total costs of production along the way—the pesticides used, the poisons released, the miles driven, the sweatshops created, and other, broader human consequences of goods and services.

Many of us now look at the clothes we wear and wonder about the conditions at the factories where they were made. Did the tiny hands of children stitch our shirts and pants? Were the workers compensated fairly? Were they forced into labor? Or, we wonder, where did this plastic bottle come from? Why is it made of this material? The answers—often harsh—change our feelings about these products and lead us to yet another, crucial question: Are there better options?

It's become clear that the way people have lived and produced for the past century cannot continue. Such behavior is simply not sustainable. A whole industry has grown around this revelation as products and businesses are being built on a smarter framework of ecological, economic, and social sustainability. This new outlook has other critical components: personal, cultural, and communal sustainability. Economic towers are built on solid social foundations. Long-lasting strength and stability come when

Textiles often have symbolic uses, and certain motifs have great significance. For example, in Laos, a young woman can still show her love for a young man by weaving him a small handkerchief. To this day, weavers take shawls used by shamans during healing rituals and use them to make wedding blankets. The geometric patterns and symbols, such as dragons and birds, believed to aid the shaman in healing are also believed to protect the young couple from evil spirits and bring them good luck. Other motifs, such as the snake, appear in textiles and other cultural objects in Cambodia, Thailand, and Laos. In Cambodia, it occurs often throughout the temple complex of Angkor Wat. The serpent also offers protection of the home and helps safeguard the rice harvest.

The looms I saw on my visit with Anh had ornately sculpted wooden parts, constructed with great care from local trees. The women talked while their deft fingers set the warps with colorful thread in a method passed down through generations. Being in their orbit made me feel at ease, mesmerized by their intricate work. Many weavers described the work as meditative; it fit into their daily lives and set a cadence—a movement of body, of time, of life. However, in reality, despite the calm, these people lived precariously. As farmers and weavers, they depended on their crops' success and the fabric they sold in the village or market just to get by. Financially, it was unpredictable. Economic desperation makes some families vulnerable to human traffickers, who promise jobs or

the person and the place are treated with dignity and respect. As we rise from the mire of decades of unsustainable consumption, we find that the most fulfilling goods and services are those that connect us in relevant ways to other people and help us live more in concert with our own values.

This new way of thinking is revolutionizing the business of design and the design of business, turning "consumers" back into "customers" and uniting us all through our shared human experiences. Many designers are realizing that they, too, have a responsibility and a desire to create sustainable and holistic products and services—and that this goal requires an equally sustainable, sensitive, and sensible product-development process. Designers envision a new form of systemic design, in which each part complements and cleanly integrates into the whole. They see design not as something added to "pretty up" a product but rather as an integral part of the larger process of problem solving. Ultimately, design is no longer regarded just as a profession—something that architects, product designers, textile designers, industrial designers, and graphic designers do once they have a portfolio and degree. Design is now understood as an approach, a way to view the world and create an ongoing lifestyle. This awakening took decades, and for many designers it was not an easy shift. Formerly, designers rarely thought about or engaged all parts of the whole. Complex projects were broken other prospects only to ensnare men, women, and children in sweatshops, brothels, and bonded labor. My future trips to Southeast Asia would put me face-to-face with the horror and sadness of the slave market. I also came to understand how fair wages, education, and community support can not only sustain the weavers' craft but also protect them from exploitation. This focus helped shape my commitment to the region as much as my fascination with its textiles. But on that first trip, my mind and heart were captured only by the weavers and their artistic traditions.

Although the setting couldn't have been more foreign, as a designer I was struck by a feeling of creative camaraderie with the weavers. Their stories, their warmth, and their exquisite artistry enthralled me. I loved the interconnected, mutual support of the community. Everyone had a job and a purpose, and they all took deep pride in their work. Also, every home in these farming villages had at least one loom. Children grew up around them and learned to use them. Weaving was not just an activity that provided income beyond farming, I realized. It held deep cultural significance.

Surrounded by the methodical sound of the shuttle carrying the thread back and forth between the warp and the mesmerizing sight of the spinning wheels, my mind, too, began to spin.

up into discrete parts and assembled later. Some designers didn't even know they were designing the components of a larger system.

In the past decade or so, leading thinkers in a range of professions and circumstances have explored these changes, with powerful results. We see the paradigm of design being redefined by savvy nonprofits, such as Paul Polak's D-Rev and Cameron Sinclair and Kate Stohr's Architecture for Humanity, as well as for-profit businesses, such as William McDonough and Michael Braungart's MDBC. Journalists and other writers are sharing stories of innovative business models, as Nicholas Kristof and Sheryl WuDunn do in their book, *Half the Sky: Turning Oppression into Opportunity for Women Worldwide*. In the world of finance, Jacqueline Novogratz's nonprofit Acumen Fund invests in entrepreneurs working to fight global poverty. And people can also be innovators in their own backyards: William Kamkwamba—who tells his story in *The Boy Who Harnessed the Wind: Creating Currents of Electricity and Hope*—started out building a windmill to harness energy for his family's house in Malawi. He then brought their village its first drinking water via solar-powered pump.

Many important business and design experts have begun to look deeply at systemic change, which is encouraging not only a new class of entrepreneur but also a new kind of

DISRUPTIVE ENTREPRENEUR
PATRICK AWUAH / ASHESI UNIVERSITY

Patrick Awuah left a successful high-tech career at Microsoft to return to his native Ghana, believing the young people of his home country needed to develop foundational skills in critical thinking, leadership, and ethical service—essential values for building a strong and prosperous nation. In 2002, he founded Ashesi University (ashesi means "beginning" in Fanti, one of Ghana's native languages) and is charting a new course in African education.

I first came to the United States for school when I was twenty. It didn't occur to me then that I would return to Africa, to Ghana, after my schooling. I would go back to visit but felt more compelled to stay in the U.S. for work. But after my son was born, I felt a pull back to Ghana, to make a difference there. So for a while I was living between these two worlds.

For too long, I knew, the people of Ghana had accepted the status quo of poverty, illiteracy, and corruption, and I wanted to help break that cycle. Wouldn't it be great, I thought, if we could teach the next generation of leaders the skills that would foster deep ethical values, as well as critical thinking and problem-solving skills? That would mean

academic training. The number and variety of social entrepreneurship courses offered by business schools has increased dramatically over the last ten years. Most MBA programs now offer some classes, while several of the world's top-ranked institutions— including Stanford University, Oxford, New York University, Spain's ESADE, and Harvard—have dedicated programs and concentrations in this new field. Design schools also are adding classes and programs in sustainable design and design thinking, recognizing this imperative role. Many of these design and business schools are expanding their programs as businesses expand the role of design to encompass all aspects of their companies.

These programs appeal especially to a generation raised in a world where easily accessible global communication and widely opened global markets make the next hemisphere seem as close as the next county. Tens of thousands of miles evaporate with each text message, e-mail, or Skype call, and with this new connectivity comes enhanced opportunity. Social problems around the world no longer seem so removed from our own. We see ourselves in other people's struggles and stories. We see our families and friends. We are these stories.

improving and overhauling our education system. If we could teach a new generation of business leaders and doctors and lawyers and judges to work with a new set of values, we could truly have a transformative national experience. That is what inspired me.

In order to do this, I wanted to create a school based on student-centered learning, and where the instructor guided students through a process of discovery. The challenges for the students would be analytical and creative, but the academic program would need to be built on a sense of ethos, values, and integrity. This makes a huge difference, because we are training future leaders to be ethical and compassionate beings; people who can run the country with competence.

I was thirty-five and working at Microsoft when I brought up the idea of starting a school overseas. My co-workers were very enthusiastic. No one tried to talk me out of it. This was during the days of the dot-com boom, and there was a lot of excitement about life in general. People thought my opening a school in Ghana was a wild idea, but they also encouraged me to follow my dream.

When you start any enterprise, you steadily build a team, gather resources, and execute a plan. But the stakes felt very high for me. In the beginning, I was very afraid that I

THE LULAN STORY

The dusty motorbike trip I took to the weaving village outside Hanoi in 1992 started a journey that led, after many twists and turns, to my developing Lulan Artisans. Founded in 2004, Lulan is a for-profit social venture that designs, produces, and markets contemporary textiles through partnerships with artisans in Southeast Asia. We sell fabric as yardage, finished home-furnishing products (such as pillows, duvets, throws, table runners, and placemats), and accessories (such as scarves, shawls, purses, wallets, phone cases, and computer cases). We market these products to interior designers through showrooms and on Lulan.com. We sell to retail customers online or through our showroom in Charleston, South Carolina, and wholesale through specialty stores such as ABC Carpet and Home.

Lulan's mission is to join high design with traditional weaving techniques while honoring the artisans' social and cultural heritages. We work with more than 650 spinners, dyers, weavers, and finishers in Cambodia, Laos, Thailand, Vietnam, and India. Our gifted artist partners spin the fibers, dye the threads, and weave the cloth. Their looms are hand built, their raw materials naturally grown. One of our main objectives is to create jobs in these communities. By providing people with economic options, human trafficking can be prevented and communities can become more stable.

would fail. To manage my fear and minimize the chances of failure, I decided to go to business school to learn more skills, which I did. And this experience helped immensely. Twelve years ago, when I first began to think about this venture, it was just a couple of people and me. By 2002, we had thirty students and a couple of faculty members. Now, we have 500 students, a staff of about seventy, and approximately 200 graduates. So we've grown from one person working on this project—me—to hundreds.

Our graduates do very well. They achieve 100 percent placement in jobs and grad school within six months of graduation. Several former students have started their own companies. And they really stand out because of their education, which taught them to be problem solvers, so they're in very high demand.

Despite these successes, we are also realists. We take the long-term view of how all of this will play out. I hope that when my young children are in their thirties or forties, Africa will be as connected and advanced as any other continent in the world. That will be the measure of our success. That is what drives me forward.

My years of in-depth work with our weaving partners have taught me that true sustainability has six key components, which Lulan highlights: ecological, economic, social, cultural, communal, and personal. Our artisans are earning a living wage and discovering new business opportunities for their skills and products. Lulan goes even further, discerning the specific needs of the individual communities and offering tailored benefits, such as education and housing allowances. The benefits vary from place to place because people pick the benefits that work best for them as a group. This helps strengthen the community in the short and long term. Individuals who see the effects of these benefits personally can value them even more collectively.

One of Lulan's primary goals is to effect systemic social change. We are creating not just a set of well-crafted textiles or even a viable model for artisanal products, but something larger: an ecosystem solution that works at the product, service, and community levels. Our "bottom-up" philosophy invigorates ancestral artistic processes and creates value by honoring values. Our holistic approach adds purpose, meaning, and vitality to the larger cultural context. The Lulan Artisans story is one of hope, holistic sustainability, true partnerships, and long-term economic independence, involving a unique collaboration between designers and artisans within the framework of a for-profit business.

A MOVEMENT ACCELERATES

At the heart of this book are more than two dozen stories about a new world unfolding. Some of them are highly personal; a few names have been changed to respect the teller's privacy. I interviewed all of these inspiring people in the course of writing the book. Excerpts from some of our conversations punctuate the narrative, and each chapter includes one of these stories.

These diverse accounts are but a small sampling of the many that shape the first wave of this design and business movement. These social entrepreneurs use strong business structures and principles to help solve a problem while making a profit. But perhaps "disruptive entrepreneur" is a better term for these iconoclasts, as it defines the type of individual now pushing this movement forward. Many use grassroots methods to take on critical problems such as human trafficking, poverty, and long-term health issues. There are tens of thousands of us. We do not know when the tipping point will occur, but action has begun and the movement is building. These dramatic changes rest on a number of bedrock developments, including a reimagining of the design process; the embrace of a new form of system change; stakeholder collaboration; personal, cultural, and communal sustainability; the power of storytelling; and flexible business models. All of these topics are explored in the pages that follow.

This is not a book about dreamy idealism but of real, sustainable enterprise. Businesses must make money to survive. Society must balance compassion with a greater understanding of the complexity of the issues and impacts. We have to redefine the problems, using innovative and culturally adaptive models. We are at a point where the various threads—social, cultural, financial, and others—can be successfully woven together. Collectively, we must take this movement into the business mainstream in the next five to ten years because, simply put, we don't have a choice. We must get this right. This is the future of business. This is the future of design.

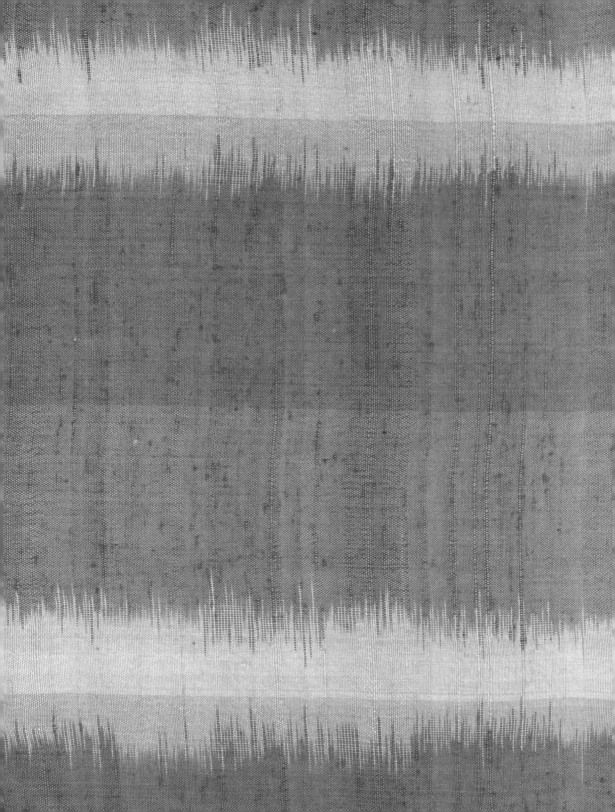

IT'S NEVER A LINEAR PATH

"Following straight lines shortens distances, and also life."

—Antonio Porchia, "Voces", 1943, translated from the Spanish by W. S. Merwin

GUIDING INFLUENCES

Since my earliest visits to the markets in Southeast Asia, I've seen many Japanese shoppers buy antique as well as new handwoven textiles. Japanese organizations and businesses still strongly support and buy from artisanal weaving groups. Not only do many Japanese know about the processes of spinning, dyeing, and weaving by hand; they also are passionate about seeing these techniques kept alive throughout developing Asian countries. This is because hand weaving, an integral part of Japan's culture for centuries, has for the most part been lost to fast-paced modernization.

Interestingly, that industrialization grew out of Japan's traditional weaving workshops. Some of the Japanese companies that are household names today got their start in textiles. Toyota was originally Toyoda Automatic Loom, an early innovator in the field. Sakichi Toyoda received his first patent in 1891 for his wooden handloom. In 1929, Platt Brothers & Co. of England bought the rights to Toyoda's Type-G automatic loom. With those proceeds, Toyoda started the Toyota Motor Co. Mitsubishi was also heavily engaged in the fiber industry. Countrywide, Japanese textiles represented about one third of

DEEP-ROOTED DESIGN

Starting a company begins a journey that, almost immediately, broadens and transforms from what you first set out to do. It's rarely a linear path. It sometimes takes years to put all the pieces in place and to seize opportunities as they unfold.

Careers are also not linear. After my initial, exploratory travel in Southeast Asia in 1992, I went to business school and then returned to Vietnam for two years to work. I came back to the United States in 1996, just as the Internet boom was beginning. I quickly landed a job as vice president of business development with the 3-D entertainment company Gravity (later purchased by Frog Design). With my experience in business development and the new emerging online market, I wanted eventually to start a company to put the weavers' work on the Web and introduce them to a wider customer base.

During this gold rush period of Internet business startups—when venture capital was plentiful and companies launched by the thousands—it was widely believed that thinking big was essential. As such, advisors and mentors considered my idea for selling artisanal work online too narrow. They urged me to enlarge my vision, and so I created Envolved, an Internet company focused on new interactive ways to inspire, the country's production in the 1930s. But by the late 1970s, Mitsubishi, like others, felt the pressure of international competition and started to diversify production beyond textiles.

Women have always played a leading role in the story of Japan's fiber arts, and traditional garments such as the kimono continue to have symbolic significance within the culture. Many Japanese have some connection to textiles and can tell you a story or two about its influence on their family.

Joi Ito—entrepreneur, venture capitalist, former CEO of Creative Commons, and director of the MIT Media Lab—is one of those people. Joi grew up within a strong matriarchal family. For the past seventeen generations, when men in the family have died, women have taken over. After World War II, Joi's great-grandmother set up the first textile trade school for women in northern Japan—a radical innovation, despite the significant participation of women in the Japanese textile industry during its beginnings and early industrialization. The family house was connected to the school. When Joi's great-grandmother died, in the late 1960s, his grandmother took over. She built a day-care center and a trade school for nurses. The school remained a pillar of education in the region through the 1980s. But just as Japan's economy developed and transitioned

//

connect, and donate money to a broad variety of philanthropic causes. It was early 1999, long before social media hit the mainstream. Envoled devolved, like many other Internet companies, during the rapid economic contraction of 2000. The dot-com balloon burst, venture capital dried up, the stock market plummeted, and, like many others, I found myself surrounded by the fallout in California. So much was lost, but much was also learned, and the experience would be invaluable for my future business endeavors.

My response was to return to Southeast Asia whenever possible, often for three or four weeks at a time. I moved to Charleston, South Carolina, in 2001 and continued to research, advise, and stay connected to artisan cooperatives. Charleston was an ideal place to incubate a business like Lulan Artisans, because the city was in the middle of an artisanal renaissance. The American College of the Building Arts, for instance, was created to apprentice artisans who could assist in rebuilding after the devastation of Hurricane Hugo in September 1989. I loved living in a city full of historic architecture and committed to using artisanal skills to preserve its design legacy. Charleston was also a supportive environment for starting a business. I received a loan almost immediately from the Charleston Local Development Corporation (similar to the Small Business Administration). It was important to launch Lulan in the United States, a market I was familiar with, and then expand from there.

away from textiles as a core industry, the school's focus changed as well and eventually it closed.

Joi's mother, who had the biggest impact on his life, was a CEO, also rare for a woman in Japan. She spent half of her life working in the nonprofit sector and the other at the helm of the Japanese subsidiary of Energy Conversion Devices. Joi's father was a chemist and scientist, and his family has always valued education. Yet Joi was never a formal learner, getting more from computers than the classroom. In the 1980s in Chicago, he dropped out of college to be a disc jockey in the city's nightclubs. The interaction among musicians, gangsters, police, runaways, and the homeless produced a close-knit group where every one took care of one another. Joi learned so much informally that he started to question traditional education, authority, and ownership of ideas. As a dj, he promoted and shared the hundreds of records he received from musicians. His participation in organic, self-organizing groups around the club scene—a peer-to-peer learning system that was undervalued at the time—informed his thinking and eventually led him to participate with Creative Commons.

After moving to Tokyo, Joi—always interested in computer networking—set out on his path as an entrepreneur by helping sell groupware products and launching a computer

COMMUNITY AS DESIGNER

Back in 1992, as I stood mesmerized by the weavers under the houses raised on stilts, I began to understand the concept of the artisan village. At the time, Vietnam still had more than 1,500 handicraft villages. They produced everything from drums to stone carvings to bamboo furniture and, in the process, maintained the country's rich heritage. Their crafts appealed to my personal and professional sense of design. Years earlier, I had received my master's degree in architecture from Tulane University, and later, while working at Gensler in Los Angeles, I helped design buildings and interior spaces for companies such as IBM and Sony. Gensler was a great place to work and learn technical, design, and management skills. But unlike other architects, I wasn't excited about large-scale projects. Textiles touched me in ways that glass-and-steel megaprojects never did. There was a foundational design and structure to textiles that felt personal and immediate. Discovering the weavers awakened in me a longing to design in this intimate, complex medium—something used every day that also expresses a culture, a design you can hold in your hand and brush across your cheek.

I decided to move from design in an architectural practice to a new model of design partnership, in which artisans aligned themselves with sophisticated markets to sell their remarkable goods more widely. A few artisan villages had toeholds in the design firm. A frequent traveler, Joi feels not so much Japanese or American but more part of a broader "we." Participating as a trustee of Nishimachi International School in Tokyo, he's seen how international schools play a role in creating global citizens with sensibilities similar to his own. This global group, fueled by the technology that increasingly connects us all, is right now becoming a substantial bloc of people who can work together to effect social change.

The most influential people throughout Joi's life have been women, and this is clearly reflected in the priorities he has set for himself: support for women's rights; commitment to entrepreneurship; promoting education; and creating social impact. As he has done so far, Joi, a Lulan advisor, will no doubt continue to pursue these priorities as he continues on his nonlinear path.

DISRUPTIVE ENTREPRENEUR
DR. JORDAN KASSALOW / VISIONSPRING

Dr. Jordan Kassalow is the founder and CEO of VisionSpring, which provides affordable eyeglasses and business opportunities in the developing world. He received his doctorate of optometry from the New England College of Optometry and his master's in public health from Johns Hopkins University.

arts-and-crafts world, where their work was sold as "fair trade." But I began to envision something different. Arts and crafts was not the right positioning for them. Instead, I thought, we should pair the skills of the artisans and the quality of their products with modern design markets, thus creating bold new opportunities for their own businesses. It quickly became apparent that a traditional fabric company was not an adequate structure for this endeavor. It would be better to create a larger, more world-savvy version of the weaving community—a container for collaboration among generations of skilled artisan families, but connected to a wider audience.

Designer Dawn Danby manages the Sustainable Design Program at Autodesk, creator of design software such as AutoCAD. She states, "Design can be an integral part of improving communities, provided it's not something that is imposed from the outside." She also describes a structure wherein the community, in fact, becomes the designer. "It creates an opportunity for people in the community to be involved and work on projects." This has widened the range of individuals who are involved in design.

Determined to explore this idea of community as designer, I began to visit other weaving communities in Southeast Asia. I wanted to see how this traditional craft fit into people's everyday lives and how it varied—or didn't—across boundaries of villages,

When I was first studying to be a doctor of optometry, I joined a student group called Volunteer Optometric Services to Humanity. We set up clinics to provide eye care in underserved areas in the world. For many people, it was the first eye care they had ever received. On my inaugural trip, we went to a small rural town in the center of the Yucatán Peninsula in Mexico. My first patient was a seven-year-old boy from a local school for the blind, and I knew pretty quickly that his problems went beyond my expertise. So I called my professor over, and after a good long look, she said, "Jordan, this boy isn't blind." He was just profoundly myopic, and it could be corrected. Here was a child who simply needed a really strong pair of glasses.

We had brought a box of about 5,000 glasses with us, and we put the strongest prescription on him. Suddenly, the blank stare of a blind child transformed into this incredible, universal smile of joy. He saw the world for the first time, and I was the first person he had ever seen. We each had a transformative moment. He, in that instant, turned from a blind child into a sighted child, and I quickly learned what success was.

That happened in 1984, but I didn't start VisionSpring until 2002. During those two decades, I developed skills that I needed to feel confident in starting my own social enterprise. I spent a year working in India at the famous Aravind Eye Hospital, and

towns, cities, and even countries. There were overall constants in the region, such as ikats and brocades, but specific local differences, too. The looms were uniquely set up technically, depending on how that village had been taught. Most had traditional looms, but others had hybrids that incorporated a Swedish method for creating more consistent tension on the warp. Understanding these idiosyncrasies could influence the design of the business.

On my first trip to Southeast Asia, after visiting Vietnam I went to Cambodia. Travel there was risky, because guerilla remnants of the Khmer Rouge were targeting tourists in an attempt to show the world they still had power. The country had been eviscerated by the agrarian Communist fanaticism of Khmer Rouge leader Pol Pot in the 1970s, when an estimated 2 million people were killed outright or died as the result of torture, overwork, disease, or starvation. At the time of my trip, Cambodia was still fifteen years away from tribunals seeking justice for Pol Pot's genocidal campaign, which aimed to create a pure peasant society through forced labor, mass killings, and the elimination of religion and the educated class.

I took a boat ride up the great Tonle Sap waterway. The small wooden vessel had an enclosed area to shield some passengers from the sun and an open area for bags of food, afterward, I received my public health degree. I worked for a nonprofit called Helen Keller International, distributing Mectizan, which is a drug that treats river blindness. I learned there how to administer simple health products in faraway places. Next I spent five years at a think tank, where I worked with government and business leaders and was exposed to foreign policy on a large scale. I also started my own company selling simple reading glasses. By then, I had accumulated experience in the nonprofit sector, the foreign policy sector, and the business sector, and all that led me to start VisionSpring.

Part of our scaling strategy is to show multinationals and governments that investing in the distribution of eyeglasses has huge benefits. Our studies show that our eyeglasses increased worker productivity by 35 percent. So if you go to governments, tell the ministers of finance that if they want to increase productivity in their work force, there are some easy ways to do it, and one of them is to make sure that people can see their work. With just a $1 pair of glasses, you can increase someone's productivity by one-third for the next twenty years.

We also have a unique business model. Essentially, we provide "a business in a bag" by giving local entrepreneurs sales kits that allow them to market and sell glasses to their

animals, and more passengers. Several other foreigners came aboard. As we skimmed along, gunshots came out of nowhere. One bullet hit the side of the boat. The others hit the water. Shaken but safe, we all considered ourselves lucky.

Making my way around the country, I learned that some of the weaving communities were several hours away from the markets. When I arranged for a motorbike driver to take me to one of the infamous Killing Fields, I also asked him to take me to Takeo, a vibrant weaving region. At the time, most visitors stuck to historical sites such as Phnom Penh, Angkor Wat, the Killing Fields, and Tol Sleng, the school where the Khmer Rouge tortured and killed many Cambodians. I wasn't sure if going farther afield was safe, but I was determined to meet more artisans in my quest to understand the different weaving techniques of Southeast Asia.

So much was new in the lives of the people I met on my trips. From around 1992 to 1996, tourism went from anomaly to reality, and my travels coincided with tremendous political and economic changes in the region. The United Nations set up elections in Cambodia in 1993, a signal that tourism might soon be encouraged. And the lifting of the U.S. trade embargo against Vietnam in 1994 and full normalization of trade the following year opened the country to Western commerce for the first time in decades. These neighbors. These "vision entrepreneurs" undergo three days of training in basic eye care and business management, and receive close, ongoing support from our staff. "Vision entrepreneurs" also partner with local schools and churches to provide outreach on vision care and offer screenings.

The design of the glasses is an important part of our success. We design our products based on what our customers want, because we're asking them to spend money on the product. It may not be much to us, only three or four dollars, but it could be 10 percent of their monthly income.

When we started to work with community groups and microfinance institutions, we didn't know, culturally, if there was going to be a demand for these glasses or whether people would trust their neighbors as our vision entrepreneurs; one day these people were simply neighbors, the next they would be eye doctors. And many of them would be women. So we did a lot of testing to see what kind of cultural barriers might exist, what kind of reception women would get, how easily we could train the women, and whether they would be able to responsibly distribute the glasses. We had other cultural concerns, too. In some countries, it's hard for a woman to travel on her own. So now our female entrepreneurs often have their husbands go to other communities nearby.

widespread shifts impacted the weavers as well as many businesses in the region. Some weavers, for instance, were already working their looms year-round, but more began to do so, leaving the rice harvest behind. Others would always continue to help during the main planting season and spend the rest of the time weaving.

BOLD COLORS, BOLD IDEAS
For several years, I continued to visit the weaving centers and each time felt the same intoxication as during that first visit. One bright morning, during a return trip to a village in Cambodia, I was hit with the sudden clarity that I needed to build a business with these communities. My background in architecture, design, business development, and marketing had prepared me to start a textile business in partnership with master artisans. It was exactly what I wanted to pursue, but timing is important, and I still had groundwork ahead. During the years between my decision to start this business and the actual launch of Lulan, I learned about the weaving process and built solid relationships with the weavers. These relationships would form the backbone of the company.

I began to think of design in a more overarching sense, not just as a concept of functionality but also as a means of forming a new business. "We're starting to see the role of design being applied more broadly, not just to objects but also to how we solve

In general, collaborations and partnerships are keys to our success. We work with groups such as BRAC in Bangladesh, which sells simple health products like home-birthing kits, oral dehydration salts, sanitary napkins, adhesive bandages, and aspirin. We started offering these products as well as eyeglasses so that the women have more goods to sell and can earn a living. It helped us reach a break-even point more quickly. There are a lot of products and services that people need. One of the challenges is to define exactly what you are going to provide and how you are going to do it effectively.

I still remember the moment when we put glasses on that child in the Yucatán and, for the first time in his life, he could see. In some respect, we are trying to replicate that moment many times over. If we can do that, we will have a very meaningful and successful impact on many lives.

///

particular logistical problems," Danby explains. She recalls a project she worked on, for instance, that focused on decreasing the energy and carbon emissions impacts of local food distribution. "We solved a lot of challenges for local farmers when we looked at the issues as a design problem," she explains. "In the end, what we built was more robust—a full business and execution plan. The design process we used questioned whether this was a viable business. And it was extremely valuable for that. I've seen more and more designers think of themselves as entrepreneurs."

In considering my idea, the designer in me could identify the need for some significant changes. For all of their magic, the weavers, naturally, lacked a deep understanding of modern design aesthetics. The fabrics coming off their looms were too bright and busy for the typical buyer. Designs that sold in international markets used subtle but sophisticated tone on tone, like light gray with dark gray, or shades of complementary colors. When some of the weavers of Southeast Asia tried to design for other markets, they would make a solid blue scarf or modify their traditional designs slightly. This resulted in only modest success, because the designs were still too intricate. Simplifying the designs would not only make them more appealing to international buyers but sometimes would allow a weaver to create more yardage in less time. Aside from some design shifts, a successful collaboration with these groups would require production changes, such as wider fabrics and color consistency, in order to meet the demands and requirements of potential new customers.

In the early 1990s, fair trade was a niche market. The demand for sustainable fabrics—and the sustainability movement itself—was nascent. I was uncertain that market demand would match the weavers' output. Even if the weaving groups could modify some of their design and production standards, the international market was not substantial enough to provide livelihoods for many artisan communities. In short, it was not yet time for me to start a formal partnership with the weavers in the early 1990s. Instead, with great excitement, I was preparing to go to business school.

A SHIFT IN FOCUS

Having already graduated with a master's in architecture, I decided to pursue an MBA to round out my design and business skills. In the fall of 1992, I entered business school in San Francisco. At the time, there were few curricula around social entrepreneurship, and even now there is no magic program that prepares one for starting a new venture. Business school was instructive, but it couldn't teach me about the type of business I wanted to put together: design-centric, grassroots, collaborative, and socially innovative. I felt my architectural background was more instructive in these areas. I had always been drawn to humanistic design philosophies, such as the people-centered designs of Craftsman homes or Eames chairs, and saw that the weavers' artisanal work—with its natural materials, human scale, and tactile, intimate physicality—was exactly that.

My visits to the weaving villages had excited my passion for the project, and business school gave me an awareness of the nitty-gritty practicalities involved in running a company. At the start of every school break, I dashed back to Hanoi to work any odd job I could get. I wanted to see the dramatic changes the country was undergoing as it shifted from a socialist-oriented economy to a market economy—a process the Vietnamese call *doi moi,* or "change and openness," an idea similar to the Russian perestroika.

Five weeks shy of receiving my MBA, I took a job in Hanoi with a Singaporean woman. She had started an interior design magazine for Vietnam, as well as a full-service interior design company. She wanted me to help her renovate old French villas into office space for companies like Chase Manhattan and Price Waterhouse. She needed me in Hanoi because she planned to open another office in Ho Chi Minh City. This was a great opportunity in general, and I was especially eager to live in Hanoi. The lightning pace of economic change in Vietnam made it an exciting time in history to be there. I left school in November 1994 for a job that would take me back to a land I loved. I was heading to Hanoi.

REACH DEEP, REACH OUT

Before I launched Lulan, I spent thirteen years researching, advising, and building artisan relationships. Indirectly, I was slowly designing a business. Looking back, I now know that taking so much time to build a company is not unusual, especially for one with cultural and social goals. Slowly and organically establishing the business model in partnership with the artisans from the ground up was too important to rush.

I looked at the weavers' skills and considered the market. What were the limitations for them? Yardage was still one. The fabric coming off their traditional looms maxed out at 39 inches in width. But the standard widths for textiles in Canada, Europe, and the U.S. are closer to 54 or 55 inches. We needed to make our fabric as wide as possible for the industry but still respect the weaver. Certain widths are not doable when throwing the shuttle manually. The easiest width is the span of your arms when you stretch them out sideways, parallel to the ground. Plus, the material loses width when it's washed. We needed to find a solution. So, like most designers, we started doing prototypes. One group of weavers could make 45 inches right away, while many could produce only 40. We tinkered with the looms, making them slightly wider. After some tweaks, we were able to set our manual-loom standard at 42 inches—45 at most for silk. Semiautomatic looms allowed weavers in some regions or countries to produce 54 to 55 inches.

LULAN ARTISANS

With relationships nearly a decade and a half in the making, it was finally time to officially form the company. In early 2003, I incorporated Lulan Artisans. Loulan was a city on the Silk Road in China, and I loved the sound of the name. I simplified the spelling and added the word *artisans* to show that the company's focus was on the craftspeople. Over the next year, I set up the company logistically, designed the first collection with textile consultants Laura Guido-Clark and Michael Koch, received the first design and color samples, oversaw the production of fabric, renovated a showroom space in Charleston, and developed a market strategy.

To move ahead, I solidified partnerships with twelve of the weaving cooperatives and groups I had been meeting with repeatedly since the early 1990s. These groups, located in villages and towns in Cambodia, Laos, Thailand, and Vietnam, had already demonstrated strength in organizing themselves as for-profit or nonprofit cooperatives. Many had an effective leader or leaders who worked well together. Some had dyeing, weaving, and spinning teams that used local natural fibers—such as silk, cotton, linen—obtained either by farming the materials themselves or buying them from nearby producers. Most primarily sold traditionally designed fabrics to local markets, although several had begun selling products internationally.

Every weaving group signed a contract with Lulan. This was a new concept to many of the collectives, but it was essential for them to learn and practice international industry standards. Each contract outlined dye lot parameters (the permissible variation in color); the financial deposits weavers would receive to run their end of the business; standards for packing and shipping; custom and duty requirements; and quality and design standards (using approved weaving samples and a description of what would constitute low quality in design, materials, or finishing methods that Lulan could not accept). The contracts also included language to guarantee that the cooperatives worked in agreement with Lulan's philosophy of sustainability in six areas: ecologically, economically, socially, culturally, communally, and personally.

Lulan's artisans used a variety of designs and colors. I had spent years gathering samples of what each weaving group could do. Laura, Michael, and I designed specifically for their capabilities, using techniques integrated with patterns and colors in ways that would sell in international markets. To guide us, I created a design brief, a detailed document stating the collection's overall objectives in terms of designs (geometric patterns, stripes, and solids); weaving techniques (ikats, brocades, and plain weaves); product end use (yardage, drapery, pillows, throws, duvets, scarves, and shawls); and cooperative skills aggregated among the different cooperatives. A design brief takes into consideration not just the design focus but also product and market strategy. The final collection highlighted the artisans' master skills and focused on what was unique about the weavings of each of the participating groups.

As Danby states, "Design has always been about aesthetics—and it still is, but now it includes much more. The criteria are broader. All of a sudden, there are backstories, contexts that come into play, that are combined with aesthetics." As I prepared to launch Lulan, I thought about how some people talk about applying solutions broadly—how they can scale around the world. But in most instances, design is contextual. It's about doing something appropriate for a particular place and time, for particular individuals, for a particular climate. Lulan started in four countries, engaging artisans with diverse skills in many cooperatives, and we combined aesthetics with context, culture, and story to produce one comprehensive collection, called 11/17.

Lulan debuted at the end of 2004. We entered the interior design market through showroom partners in Las Vegas, New York, San Francisco, and Seattle, and through our own showroom in Charleston. We launched our Web site to reach interior designers in other U.S. regions and to sell finished home-furnishing products to retail customers online. All the pieces were in place.

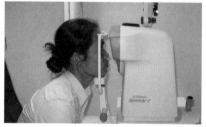

DISRUPTIVE ENTREPRENEURS

A SENSE OF PLACE

I grew up in an ordinary house on a cul-de-sac in Middletown, Ohio. At the end of a short street was a long driveway that led to a 1950s suburban ranch. I spent the first eighteen years of my life there. Some say Middletown got its name from its location: midway on the Great Miami River and halfway between Cincinnati and Dayton. Our neighborhood was a classic American suburb, more utilitarian than anything. The architecture was simple and unadorned, not very distinctive or exciting.

Nearby, however, was a house that made me very curious. It was a low, one-story structure made of wood and glass. I didn't know then that it was traditional Japanese architecture, filtered through a modernist sensibility. I only knew that it was like no place I'd ever seen. All the other houses in my neighborhood used shades or blinds or drapery over the windows for privacy. This one did not. It had an enclosed central courtyard, with a small koi pond and a beautiful green garden. I would sneak in as often as I could. The walls facing the courtyard were all glass, so I could see inside the house and notice how each room flowed into the next. An enormous tree growing there made the courtyard seem like a magical retreat in the middle of suburbia. Though I'm sure the owners saw me often enough, they never complained about my visits.

SPIRITED PROVOCATEURS

The role and definition of "design" in business has changed. A new generation of thoughtful leaders from almost every field imaginable has responded to these important changes with innovative forms of business built on insights and values and committed to making a positive difference in people's lives. These are the "disruptive entrepreneurs." Disruptive entrepreneurs are driven as much by meaning as by money, and are provocateurs who challenge traditional modes of business with insight and tenacity. There are untold tens of thousands of us around the world—and our number is growing.

We come from diverse backgrounds, religions, and cultures. We speak different languages. You'll find we are young and old, rich and poor, college educated and virtually unschooled. Some of us travel far to help, while others effect important change in our own village or region. We collaborate, excite, inspire, create, include, modify, adapt, and redefine. Open-minded, open-sourced, optimistic, and passionate, disruptive entrepreneurs feel part of a bigger world—a world of equal individuals ready to engage in any business model, with any stakeholder, in any partnership that advances transformative social change today and for future generations.

As I grew older, I began to realize why I loved this space so much. It was the intimacy, the balanced proportions, the human scale, the integration of nature, the integrity of materials, the openness of the plan, and the way that all the pieces came together to form a harmonious whole. It had such a sense of place. It felt balanced, meditative, and safe, and through it I began to understand and appreciate the power of design. Spending time in that courtyard, so aesthetically removed from the rest of the neighborhood, felt extraordinary.

Years later, after becoming a trained architect, I often recalled those times in the courtyard and the lessons I learned there. I promised myself I would try to create things with that same sensibility. In this quest, I wandered far from the small cul-de-sac in Middle America. Traveling, I would experience a world shifting to find its own sense of place, and I realized that sometimes you have to disrupt the status quo in order to establish harmony and balance.

DISRUPTIVE ENTREPRENEUR
JULIANA ROTICH / USHAHIDI.ORG

Juliana Rotich is the program director of Ushahidi.org, a nonprofit technology company initially developed to track reports, via Internet and mobile phone, of ethnic violence in

OUR RESPONSE, OUR ABILITY

Disruptive entrepreneurs recognize that traditional business models must be replaced by holistic models. We are compelled to solve large challenges and we are responding, amassing the people and skills to take action like never before in history. Unlike mainstream organizations, governmental bodies, or large corporations, disruptive entrepreneurs are capable of nimble, collaborative change. Working in decentralized but networked and partnered groups allows us to effect change more successfully. The overwhelming urgency of the world's problems is too great for outmoded business methods to keep up.

What are we disrupting? Old design methods, old business models, old processes, old thinking. Global access, global competition, and global communications have accelerated beyond the capabilities of traditional business. When economic and social changes occur, their effects are felt faster and more broadly in our interconnected world—which is disruptive on its own. It takes disruptive entrepreneurs to respond proactively to improve lives and communities as the world changes. We cannot sit back and watch economic and environmental catastrophes diminish our future quality of life. We must put in place innovative models to counteract and prevent further negative developments.

Kenya but which now is used the world over. Today, Ushahidi—which means "testimony" in Swahili—specializes in developing free, open-source software that allows information collection, visualization, and mapping for conflicts and crises the world over. More than 12,000 people have downloaded the app to their computer or phone, and more than 1.8 million have logged into the Ushahidi system.

Our idea is to gather and spread information that would otherwise not be shared, using everyday technology: e-mail, SMS, the Web, and Twitter. In many ways, Ushahidi is a direct product of online culture. It's a simple but powerful testament to what happens when you link a couple of nerds with the Internet. We are also busting the myth that a technology company cannot rise out of Kenya or even out of Africa. The initial motivation behind Ushahidi was to make sure that people in rural areas who only have mobile phones could still have their voices heard. Along the way, we became accidental humanitarians. It might be hard to believe, but we didn't set out with a big, sweeping goal. We wanted to make a difference in our own country but soon realized that our project design was relevant worldwide. So we decided to make it an open-source tool, because we believe the best way to have an impact is to innovate transparently and make successful solutions free and available.

The extreme flexibility of disruptive entrepreneurs allows us to work with established governments, businesses, and organizations. We also can improvise, selecting and combining elements from all of these systems to create new and effective models for positive impact. We modify, adapt, and try again. Disruptive entrepreneurs are proponents of "impatient change," or change that won't wait. As societal needs and wants bubble up to the surface everywhere, more people feel the imperative to generate change themselves and not wait for organizations or those with financial capital to get involved. Disruptive entrepreneurs work tirelessly to move things forward. We turn to social and cultural capital, supercharged with telecommunications tools, to mobilize people and resources and channel support in the right directions. Yet this type of change is not easy; reaching certain goals takes time and many iterations. Given the range of our backgrounds and experiences, disruptive entrepreneurs work in a variety of ways.

Boomerang change

These entrepreneurs learn effective practices by living in another country or working within a foreign system, exposed to different models, processes, and services. They then return to their countries of origin, permanently or temporarily, to enact change. Often culturally driven, they feel a sense of connection and responsibility to their homelands. These individuals respond to crises with grassroots social entrepreneurship.

One of the earliest deployments of Ushahidi was by the news organization Al Jazeera. It used our platform to visualize data about the Gaza crisis during 2008–2009, including casualties, aid deployments, protests, and Israeli rocket attacks. Vote Report India tracked developments in India's 2009 general elections. Cuidemos el Voto helped monitor incidents and irregularities via text message, e-mail, and Twitter during Mexico's election that same year. In the hours and days after the 2010 earthquake in Haiti, Ushahidi teams compiled information from journalists, local agencies, and also from individuals sending SMS messages. This running stream of grassroots reporting—about missing persons and emergency needs for food, water, and security—was then plugged into an online map so rescue and relief teams could respond more efficiently. We know from these and other success stories, including use of the Ushahidi system to map the earthquake and tsunami crisis in Japan, that people in a crowd are not just passive bystanders but instead crucial agents in providing information.

It comes down to this. People aren't waiting for the government to solve problems, since they now have the technological tools for social impact. Software helps democratize information, and the Internet is eroding barriers that once kept people from sharing their stories. It's harder for governments to get away with things. People feel empowered. They want to say, "This is how I can make a change, and now let's get on with it."

Sidestepping static, established organizations, they instead partner with people on the ground, using their own initiative and making a significant difference. The most successful of these individuals become leaders who seek out peers for support, guidance, and ideas, working with like-minded organizations as collaborators whenever possible.

Patrick Awuah, who left Ghana for the United States to attend Swarthmore College, is a great example. After a career at Microsoft, he returned to his homeland to start Ashesi University, designed to educate young people in critical thinking, ethical service, and leadership—values he believes are crucial for the nation building that lies ahead for Ghana and other African countries. Awuah is one of the many who see opportunity and use their significant skills to do something creative and positive. His experience in the U.S. empowered him to bring his knowledge back home.

Homegrown change

Disruptive entrepreneurs also effect dramatic change locally. They understand their countries' problems intimately. They recognize the need for change and feel empowered to achieve it themselves. The impact of a crisis often brings this awareness to the surface, and these renegades step into action. They know the necessary change won't happen if they wait for government or business—or that help that does come will be too slow.

The community we're building around Ushahidi is global. That comes with its own challenges, because we speak many languages, but we're united in our ability to encourage and empower each other. The tools we give to volunteers allow them to customize and deploy this technology for themselves. We also gather feedback on the different ways groups and individuals use our design. This helps us grow effectively because we find out what works where. We marvel at the way people are deploying our technology around the world, from Kenya to Mexico to Haiti. But Ushahidi is still a work in progress.

Several things are important as our company grows. First, we must have a concerted strategy for informing people about the organization. We also work with organizations on the ground that can act on the information they receive. It's important for us to partner with mobile phone companies that can either sponsor or provide the SMS for free. In many countries, sending an SMS is not free; we need to lower that cost. We also have to acknowledge the information we receive so senders know that it has been logged. Interestingly, technology is only about 10 percent of where we spend our time and effort. We devote a lot of energy to human eyes reviewing the information and determining the veracity of the data we receive.

As the number of crises—whether natural, political, or humanitarian—increases around the world, it is impossible for governments, nongovernmental organizations (NGOs), and service companies to act effectively. Limited resources, finances, and time can cost lives or impact the economic stability of a region. The homegrown disruptive entrepreneur figures out a solution based on what needs to be set into motion and then makes it happen. She is driven by a desire to keep her community strong, stable, and viable despite the difficulties. To her, a distant government agency is not as well equipped as the local community. With a core motivation not just to survive but to thrive, homegrown disruptive entrepreneurs can organize their communities, strategize, and implement solutions using local know-how and available resources. Such inspiring change is happening all over the world, in countries developed and developing, and in villages, towns, and cities of all sizes.

A prime example occurred during the devastating floods in Pakistan in 2010. The waters had divided the village of Fizagat, north of the flooded Swat Valley, halting local commerce. The villagers created a boat using recycled rubber, bamboo, and woven lattice. They built fifty of these vessels, allowing the village to reconnect and get its markets back up and running. The villagers designed their way out of crisis and into economic recovery. In times of great need, people discover inspiring solutions.

I believe Ushahidi speaks to the viability of a bottom-up versus a top-down business model. "Top down" is when big organizations parachute in and say, "Here are the solutions." We believe that more effective solutions are actually homegrown, home supported, and home empowered. We listen to what people want and to their concerns, and we respond, act, and design from there. It's important not to come with preconceived conceptions. Heaven knows we're all tired of that.

Confluent change

Disruptive entrepreneurs are keenly aware of the importance of partnering with grass-roots groups to be more effective and successful. The days of outsiders imposing their ideas and methods are over. Instead, these disruptive entrepreneurs are welcomed, because they complement and support locals in their goals and aspirations. This leads to more empowered and self-sufficient local groups that, in turn, can assist adjacent communities. Successful models of partnership can be easily adapted to fit other contexts and cultures.

Architecture for Humanity is a nonprofit design services firm that seeks solutions to global social and humanitarian crises. To date, it has seventy local chapters in over forty countries with more than 6,500 volunteer design professionals. It locally partners, collaborates, trains, educates, houses, and employs. It shares with but also learns from local communities and, in turn, distributes those lessons throughout its network of design professionals to repurpose ideas in other regions of the world. Cameron Sinclair, Architecture for Humanity cofounder and Chief Eternal Optimist (CEO), states, "It's exciting to watch what real community engagement does to the way designers think about collaboration—because we understand how to work with one another, we know it takes local, grassroots know-how."

DISRUPTIVE STRATEGIES

Disruptive entrepreneurs draw on many different concepts and strategies in their efforts to effect change. Here are some of them:

Knowledge DNA

The basic transfer of knowledge or technology between a disruptive entrepreneur and a community is simply not enough. The partnerships they create together must infuse design with innovative strategies for the community's long-term self-sufficiency. In the past, many organizations would bring in outside expertise, hiring a famous designer for a few weeks or months to assess their skill and help teach them design. But this kind of onetime exchange fails to fix underlying issues or allow local groups to really own new design processes. Such ideas need to be locally interpreted, modified, and shared in an ongoing way so they assimilate the techniques, skills, and desires of the group. Design has to live inside a creator; he has to re-envision and possess it fully for himself.

New technological, organizational, and financial tools empower networks of entrepreneurs and local communities to create novel business models and transform existing ones. These collaborations extract the best parts of old models and reassemble them into new ones. All these tools are significantly less expensive and more effective than in the past, and some are open source, putting unprecedented power in the hands of people for the first time.

The nonprofit InSTEDD helps communities design and use technology to improve health, safety, and local development. It works with governments, universities, corporations, and NGOs around the world to bridge the gap between knowledge and action for improved collaboration. For example, InSTEDD's Innovation Lab—or iLab—in Phnom Penh received start-up capital from Google to become an enterprise that provides technology-based services and products for social good. An international team of software engineers, public health professionals, and disaster responders has trained local staff to serve as a brain trust, capable of adapting technologies to suit its own needs and circumstances. In this way, iLab becomes an incubator for skills and training that can benefit all of Cambodia.

Design sprouts

If knowledge DNA describes the sharing of information between often different or unrelated groups, design sprouts are budding ideas passed from person to person, village to village. Rather than replicating or scaling a business, a design sprout allows ideas and processes to expand contextually and provides a way for people to share among themselves. When one village understands the importance of knowledge and the impact it has on its own community—for example, in learning a new method to filter safe drinking water—it often will mentor a neighboring village or community. Sometimes the potential for this type of knowledge sharing can be easy to miss. The organization Save the Children noticed that in some villages in Vietnam, a few mothers had children who did not suffer from malnutrition. It turned out that these women routinely collected small shrimp and crabs from the paddy fields to add to the children's meals. Their children were healthy, but it did not initially occur to these mothers to share this potentially vital information with others. Save the Children helped design a system of education around what these mothers were already doing naturally. The mothers taught the other women in their village, who in turn taught the next village, and the next, so that the idea ended up spreading throughout Vietnam as well as neighboring Cambodia. This design sprout made a staggering difference. The typical response to malnutrition involves the expensive import of heavy crates of rations. Here, a local solution from a local food source created sustainable change.

Hyperthinking

Ideas develop and are realized at a rate—and range—never seen before, thanks to technology and ubiquitous, real-time communication through the Internet and mobile phones. People around the world can learn about and use these tools and resources to achieve extraordinary change for themselves or within their communities. This provides a huge opportunity for designers to create even better social and cultural tools to foster and encourage the exchange of ideas. Sinclair observes, "Through technology and the use of social networking, a great idea can be a project in less than a month just by bringing together a coalition of partners."

Work matters, structure doesn't

For the disruptive entrepreneur, current business models are inadequate, and the most innovative and active organizations—whether from the corporate, government, or NGO sector—are blending, mutating, and evolving new structures. "The ends justify any means in the name of making positive change," explains Eric Corey Freed, award-winning green architect and author. "We measure success by our impact, not by how well we fit into the mold of a traditional business." The most adaptable organizations know that while their missions and values shouldn't change, their methods, structures, models, and strategies must. Disruptive entrepreneurs care about the grassroots efficacy of our impact, not the formal structure of our business. Nonprofit, for-profit—who cares? What matters is that we make a difference on the ground. It's the work that matters, not the structure.

Look out, not up

New leaders are among us in great numbers, and we stand shoulder to shoulder. No longer do leaders perch atop organizations, directing from above. We have returned to an earlier definition of a leader: one who accompanies or shows us the way. "To become truly great," noted the French political thinker Charles de Montesquieu, "one has to stand with people, not above them." This method fosters effective relationships and the open exchange of ideas—a philosophy tailor-made for the disruptive entrepreneur.

A WELL-DESIGNED SOLUTION

Sinclair makes an important observation when it comes to the intersection of design and business: "Not only can design affect business well, but the lack of design can affect business very poorly." As building blocks such as knowledge DNA become the foundation of a new generation of design, it's important to remember one critical metaview: Design isn't simply about style. The design discussed in this book is about deep, systemic engagement. There is a place for trends and styles in the world, but that approach is more ephemeral. Imagine, instead, design that responds to technological, financial, or social systems—or even the human body. Design that solves challenges across several systems satisfies more needs, coordinates more value, and marshals available resources. Systems design results in better culture and better business.

Be they financial, ecological, social, cultural, or emotional, systems already infiltrate every part of our lives. Some systems are thoughtfully designed, while others evolve through trial and error. But all systems, if they operate well, have several components in common. First, the sum is greater than the parts. A well-designed system totals more than the individual pieces. Second, the design of the system anticipates what flows through it—whether it's capital, commodities, materials, money, content, or emotions. Just as in nature, the most resilient systems are the ones with the greatest diversity; this gives them strength and enables favorable reactions from unexpected forces.

Competitive and cooperative forces are necessary for healthy, living systems to grow. This is as true for markets and organizations as it is for nature and evolution. The business world has overemphasized competition for nearly a century. Competition is still important, but without cooperation, we would be competing for peanuts instead of mindshare in a multiverse. Civilization looks the way it does—in all its wonderful, challenging complexity—because of cooperation, not in spite of it. Any well-designed system must acknowledge and address a balance between centralization and decentralization. Too much of one or the other endangers the system's resilience. Not all of these components are required, but the more you have, the more likely you will achieve a well-designed solution.

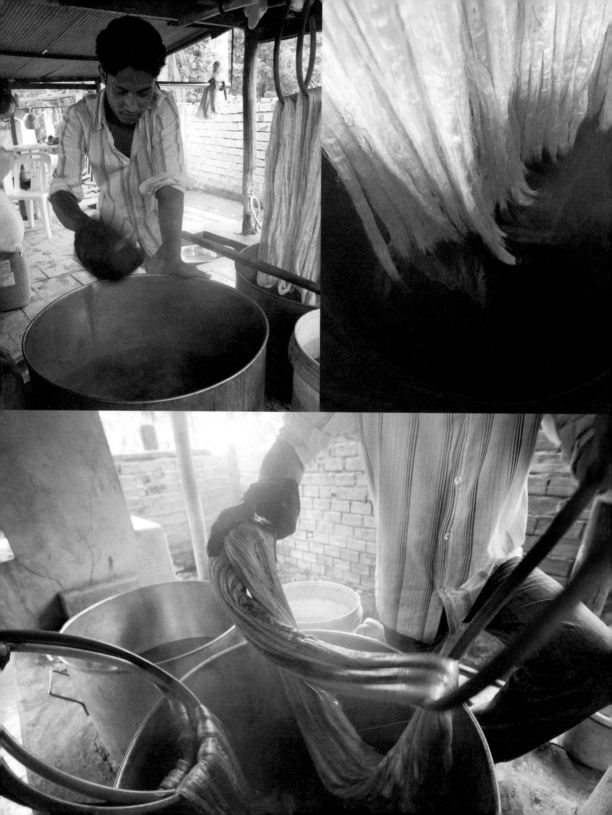

**WHAT MOVES YOU,
GRABS YOU, AND WON'T LET GO**

A FACE TO A PROBLEM

There are times when you stumble into dark spots that can suddenly change the course of your life. I had moved to Hanoi in late fall of 1994 to renovate old French villas. The city was particularly exciting at that time. I was enraptured with the crowded streets, the air filled with abrupt, lightning-fast language, and the relentless buzz of mechanized scooters zipping through narrow passageways.

I was living in a modest, family-owned hotel frequented by foreigners. The place had about twenty rooms; mine was on the second floor, overlooking an interior courtyard. During the first few months, I befriended a European who regularly visited the hotel while working for an international company. One warm evening, he and a colleague— a fellow countryman working for a large corporation—were drinking at a table facing the reception area in the lobby. When I descended the cream-colored terrazzo stairs, my friend greeted me, offered a quick introduction to his middle-aged, paunchy companion, and ordered me one of the hotel's watery cocktails. I accepted, mostly out of politeness. A few moments later, I excused myself to check at the front desk for a small package I was expecting. It had not yet arrived. As I returned, the two men were speaking their native language. Although my friend knew I speak that language, he didn't imagine it would be important to alert his friend.

IDEAS ARE NOT ENOUGH

Human trafficking is, sadly, one of the world's fastest growing criminal industries. An estimated 27 million people are being held as slaves for sex or forced labor at any one time, according to the nonprofit advocacy group Free the Slaves. Another growing criminal industry, according to Interpol, is the trade in human beings for the sale of their organs. Exact numbers are difficult to know, because many victims do not report these crimes, and with illegal trade, it's hard to calculate how much money changes hands. Yet the International Labor Organization estimates that, annually, the global profits from human trafficking are at least $39 billion. Men, women, and children are all trafficked. And this is happening almost everywhere in the world. The U.S.-based Polaris Project, which combats slavery and human trafficking, estimates that annually 200,000 American children are at high risk for sex trafficking.

During my travels, I witnessed Southeast Asia's incredible economic growth. But that amazing spike has a heartbreaking downside. As many developing countries grew rapidly, they saw a parallel surge in human trafficking, the illegal trade in human beings for the purposes of forced labor or commercial sexual exploitation. Many of these people work in factories, brothels, and on ambitious construction projects for bare wages. In many cases, they receive no money but only food and lodging. Some of the

"I'm really excited about tonight," the visiting businessman said. "I arranged to be with a Vietnamese girl later this evening." I knew about the rampant prostitution in Hanoi, so this wasn't particularly shocking. But what followed was. "Her father is arranging it," the visitor continued. "The father promises me that she doesn't have AIDS, and she's a virgin, because she's six years old."

My heart sank. My face fell. The man turned to me quickly. "You know my language," he said sharply in English, his face hardening. "Don't get involved," he warned. "This was not for you to hear or know."

My chest tightened and my mind raced. What to do? My friend said and did nothing. The drink arrived and I downed half of it quickly. I tried to act calm, but I was exploding inside. I tried, weakly, to undermine the father's claims. "They always say that, but it's not true," I countered. But my words didn't matter, so I walked away, leaving the men and the rest of my drink.

The trip upstairs to my room was a blur. Pacing around while my stomach churned, I knew I had to do something. Didn't failure to act in some way make me complicit, since I had learned about the crime beforehand? If this were the United States, a phone call

economic growth has been achieved through the exploitation of children, who perhaps have the least power to resist low pay and terrible working conditions. The proliferation of factories in urban areas, in particular, has increased the demand for slave labor—a dark byproduct of a ferocious global engine. "What I see over and over again," says Benjamin Skinner, author of *A Crime So Monstrous*, "is human traffickers leveraging the love that a parent feels for a child. To lure the child away, he'll say he'll give the child a better life." Once the child is taken away, however, all those promises of prosperity disappear.

At the core of human trafficking lies greed and corruption, orchestrated to inexpensively manufacture beautiful products that decorate our bodies and homes, construct buildings, and bring food to market. We, as buyers, are typically unaware of the frightening backstories of the products we effortlessly purchase and use. What, for instance, did it take to produce those sneakers that cost only $29.99? What about that jacket from Pakistan or the pants from Indonesia?

Slave labor is illegal in every country in the world, and yet it exists everywhere. "Businesses that are operating in the parts of the world that have the most slavery are also operating in parts of the world that have the least amount of good governance," notes to 911 would at least result in some serious questioning. But Hanoi in the mid-1990s was a different world. The burgeoning population put a strain on already meager resources, and corruption was widespread and deep rooted. Packs of motorbike thieves, for instance, often operated unchecked because the police were paid so little that they relied on bribes to feed their own families. A modest $25—in American currency—was often more than enough to buy a blind eye. However, maybe, just this once, the authorities wouldn't succumb.

I picked up the touch-tone phone in my room and was connected to the police. My heart hammered as I described where the man was. After hanging up, I closed my eyes, hoping that something would protect this little girl, wherever she was.

Hours passed. There was a knock on my door. I thought someone was dropping off the parcel I had inquired about earlier. I opened the door to find the visiting businessman staring down at me. He rushed forward, spun me around, and with one arm immobilized me in a tight, sweaty grip. In his free hand flashed the glint of a knife.

He put the blade to my throat. "I told you not to get involved," he sputtered. "Why did you think you could stop me? You knew I would only bribe the police, and I could bribe

Jolene Smith, co-founder of Free the Slaves. Smith believes that because of the entrenched nature of government practices and bureaucracy, it's up to businesses to take the lead in ending slave labor. "Businesses can move in a much more efficient way than a government can," she says. "Companies are starting to try and ensure that their supply chain is clean of slavery, since customers are interested in this issue."

At my hotel in Hanoi, I saw for myself the consequences of this human marketplace. There is a perception in many developing countries that people are merely another commodity for fueling national—and personal—dreams of progress, wealth, and power. By moving beyond the emotional horror and seeing human trafficking as a market-place—complete with all the ebbs and flows of a typical mercantile situation—I began to wonder how these market forces might be redirected. I began to think about the weavers I had met on my journeys into the countryside. Despite their cultural and aesthetic value, the Southeast Asian arts-and-crafts industries face an uncertain economic future. Artisans, whose incomes are often below poverty level, sometimes move to cities to secure jobs. And urban migration trends worldwide contribute to increased activity in human trafficking. The transition from village to city is an espe-cially vulnerable juncture, because people desperate for money are in an unfamiliar situation away from family and other support systems. "The end of slavery can't wait them more to tell me who made the call." He pulled me closer and, whispering in my ear, told me in detail what he had done to the little girl. He glared, then spun around and left. I sat there shaking, knowing I had failed both the child and myself. I felt helpless and terrified. But in that brief and unexpected moment, my life changed forever. I had moved to Vietnam as an architect of buildings. I would leave Vietnam an architect of social change.

DISRUPTIVE ENTREPRENEUR
SHAFFI MATHER / BRIBEBUSTERS.COM

Shaffi Mather set up the first successful emergency ambulance service in India, called Dial 1298 for Ambulance. His latest venture is the for-profit Bribebusters.com, designed to curtail rampant graft among Indian officials. A lawyer and TED Fellow, Mather has a degree in public policy from Harvard University and was a Chevening Gurukul Senior Scholar in Leadership and Excellence at the London School of Economics.

After moving back to India from the United States and England, I felt compelled to provide some of the basic services that Western countries and companies have but India does not. When I started the emergency ambulance project, for instance, I was asked repeatedly by officials for bribes to get the company set up. I battled this every step of

for the end of poverty," says Skinner, "but you cannot deny the absolute role of desperate poverty, underdevelopment, and social isolation in creating a readily accessible pool of potentially enslavable individuals."

Dire straits also can prompt a feverish willingness to take risks and make drastic choices. Sometimes, people bet it all to survive—and lose. In Cambodia, right before the economic downturn of 2008, farmers who had been growing silk for generations plowed their mulberry trees—the feeding ground of silkworms—in order to cultivate other crops. They hoped to cash in on the growing international market for cassava, a starchy root and widely used source of carbohydrates. Farmers in other countries also increased their supply, and the fierce competition made prices fall. That, combined with political issues with neighboring Thailand and closing access to certain markets, brought these Cambodian farmers to their knees. They fell into debt. They lost their livelihoods and, in many cases, their family land.

The fight against human trafficking requires a range of strategies. Organizations focus on awareness and education, advocacy, intervention, rehabilitation, prevention, or research. But businesses are in a powerful position to instigate and inspire change. Companies that pay fair wages and rid their supply chains of slave labor not only bolster

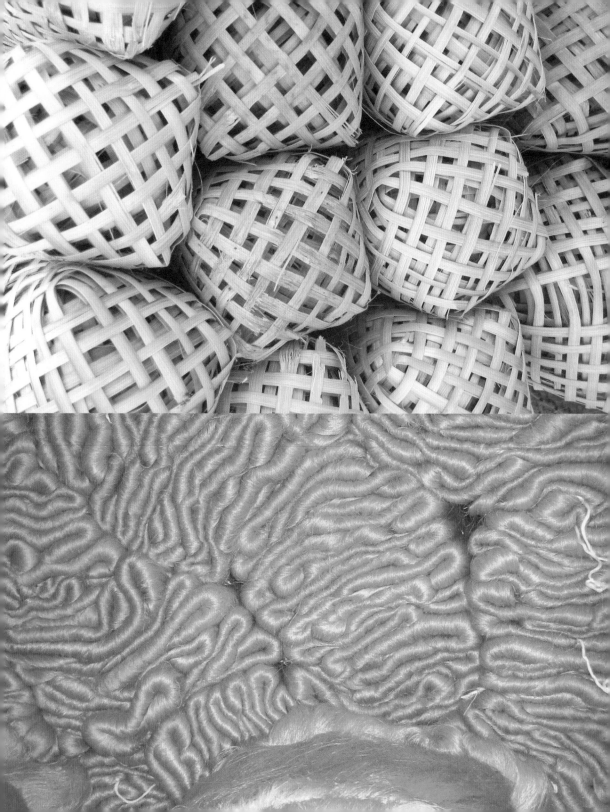

the way. There are specific trigger points in your life that create an urgency inside you, and this was one of them for me. Something had to be done. Such incidents as these led me to create Bribebusters.com, which aims to confront corruption.

Bribebusters is a professional fee-for-service organization that focuses on deterring everyday petty bribes in India. It is a consumer service for the common man, the person who is repeatedly forced to pay bribes just to get simple things done in a timely fashion. Instead of bending to this way of life and paying bribes, I wanted to create a system of empowerment that recognizes and honors integrity. A person facing a bribe can call or e-mail Bribebusters, which, for a nominal fee, will confront the corrupt official and make sure the person receives the service or procedure he or she is seeking. The Bribebusters fee is less than what the bribe would cost, so the process saves people time and money, with the larger goal of lessening systemic bribery over time.

Part of the inspiration for Bribebusters was my drive to contribute to the development of my country by playing whatever positive role I could in public policy. There were organizations that worked at the macro level—the national level, the global level—to lessen corruption. But as an individual, you had no place to go for help or recourse if you were asked for a bribe. Our service is available to anyone. We battle bribe seekers

local economies but also fuel the international market for fair-wage products. The end result, ideally, is that other companies feel the pressure and follow suit.

For my part, I decided to not just grieve for that little girl in Hanoi but to play a role in preventing human trafficking among the weavers I so admired. By increasing their incomes, and thus their stability, I believed that Lulan could lessen the likelihood that the artisans would fall prey to slave labor and other dangers. So we focus on reducing human trafficking by creating jobs. But Lulan's model also has a positive effect on other social issues. We impact education, health, and financial savings. We help decrease poverty and physical abuse. And we assist in increasing stability, respect, and community strength as a whole. Job stability improves individual and community security, which, in turn, impacts security throughout a country, a region, and, potentially, the world.

IT'S SYSTEMS DESIGN

Ultimately, the biggest questions, for me, were very simple: Could I create a sustainable business that opened up economic options for artisan communities threatened by human trafficking? And could my business model provide the weavers with steady jobs and enough money not just to survive but also to thrive and help fuel their local by putting pressure on the office where that person works. We keep pressuring until the bribe seeker feels it is better to drop the bribe demand than be exposed. We created a Hall of Fame for the good officials and a Hall of Shame for the bad ones. We use peer pressure and publicity about a certain office or a particular officer. It's a set of tools that we have found to work really well. Our fees are on a sliding scale because, in a country like India, there's a cross-section of society that may not have the ability to pay the fees equal to the time and effort of the service.

For cultural reasons, it seems easier to fight corruption in the south of India and expand from there. I think this is because of the large number of young people who have moved into IT and other services in the south. Inspired by having lived overseas or by experiencing their country's economic growth and understanding its potential, they see no reason to continue this culture of bribing people to get things done. They want no part of it.

I believe that this model of fighting bribes is replicable in all constitutional democracies. Obviously, this is not something that is going to work in a dictatorship or where constitutional rights are shaky. Globalization is moving us all toward a form of global citizenship. In India, we want systems that work for our people as well as with other economies? Business school offers a simple guideline for starting a company: Begin with what you know best—that is, do what's closest to your expertise. You can always expand into other areas after you've established a foundation and a core customer base. What I wanted to do was create a company that, while grounded in an expertise in design, was about more than just beautiful textiles. I wanted to create a viable model for artisans. Ultimately, I wanted to create a new business ecosystem solution that would work at the product, service, and community levels across economic, ecological, social, and cultural structures to make systemic change.

It was during business school that I really learned about systems design, the process of understanding how parts influence one another within a whole. This kind of thinking recognizes that a business is bigger than its individual components and that problems cannot be addressed as separate units. At the very least, it's no longer possible for organizations to continue the fiction that they are independent entities that function outside their ecosystems. This wasn't an epiphany to me. I was taught this type of integrated design in architecture school. But seeing it through the lens of business, as well as design, I realized how pervasive systems design really is and that it has broad applications in the structure of a building, a product, or a business.

countries in the world. This new world citizenship is going to be a huge challenge, because the established political interests around the globe are not going to give up easily. Ultimately, a culture of corruption wears people down. It does not create positive relationships, trust, or community. We are passionate about establishing a new structure that presents opportunities for people and a culture of goodwill. We want to use power to empower, not to abuse.

Brazil shows what can happen when a government applies systems design to solving a pernicious national problem. In early 2003, the president of Brazil, Luiz Inácio Lula da Silva, formed a commission to end slavery. His administration strengthened laws and increased funding for antislavery efforts. Any person or company caught using human slaves was put on an official "dirty list." In addition to prosecution and imprisonment, the guilty company or person was excluded from receiving government permits, grants, loans, or credits. Being denied government benefits can potentially drive slave-using companies out of business. "If a company is found to have just one slave anywhere in the supply chain, they go on that list, and the consequences are extreme," says Skinner, whose book investigates human trafficking in countries including Haiti, Sudan, Romania, and India. "It's not a good place to be, and companies work very hard to get off the dirty list."

In the design world, however, the model of systemic design is both new and foreign. The traditional way of operating followed the model of the supreme design talent who leads and drives a company or its products. Today, the profession is no longer about that kind of singular genius. It's about collaboration—a heroic, combined effort of a completely new caliber and scope.

CONTAINERS FOR COLLABORATION

A TIME TO CONNECT MORE DEEPLY

In Laos, Lulan Artisans began working with a cooperative run by a wonderful woman with terrific skills and experience. Malia's group is one of the savviest I know, and its artists continue to learn and grow at an incredible pace. She became not only a vibrant business partner but also a dear friend.

Over the years, Malia and I grew closer. Her extended family welcomed me in, and as I got to know her relatives, I was struck by how inventive and entrepreneurial they all were. During my trips to Laos, Malia took me to her temple and taught me the rituals of Theravada Buddhism. She spoke lovingly about weaving and what it means to Laos and its culture. Each visit was a delight.

One day, I went to see Malia shortly after her mother died. The loss of the matriarch was a great blow, and the family was still in mourning. Her mother had taught Malia and her sister how to weave, and with sadness and poignancy she recalled how important this woman had been to the whole family for so many years.

Perhaps driven by the raw emotion of the day, my friend began to open up and tell me her family's story. She discussed the Vietnam War, which she experienced as a child, its

CREATING YOUR CONTAINERS

When most entrepreneurs dream of building a company, they often imagine setting up an office or workspace, hiring employees, creating an infrastructure, providing unique products or services that meet orders quickly to satisfy customers—and, presto, the business is up and running. But I've learned that one of the best ways to start a new venture is to think about building not a company but a vessel, a container for collaboration in which deep relationships and partnerships flourish. This kind of company in its very nature creates an open invitation for others to participate—and is stronger as a result. Author Lisa Gansky calls these interconnected relationships "the Mesh" and has written a book with this title. "The Mesh is a fundamental embracing of the fact that we're all connected," says Gansky. "Everything is cyclical. When one benefits, we all benefit, and those who understand this interconnection will benefit the most."

This is a very different business model from fifty years ago, a time Gansky calls the Age of the Generals. "We all know the companies: General Motors, General Electric, General Dynamics. Their businesses were expensive to build, because they owned everything." These companies insulated themselves within the marketplace through their enormous investments in intellectual property and branding, and they perpetuated their domination through advertising on the three main TV channels that reached people in their impact on her country, and how the villages kept weaving during that time. She mentioned the "secret war" that U.S. forces conducted in Laos, beginning in 1964. Without the approval of Congress, the Air Force began bombing the Ho Chi Minh Trail, the supply line that brought weapons and wares to South Vietnam. The United States dropped more bombs on Laos than it did globally during World War II. As much as a third of the ordnance didn't explode, however, leaving cluster bombs embedded in the ground. Children die playing with them, and farmers seeking scrap metal to sell risk their lives searching for and digging them up. More than 11,000 people have been killed or maimed by these bombs in the nearly four decades since the conflict.

Malia's father fought with the Americans. He was in charge of a small group of soldiers who patrolled and protected the Ho Chi Minh Trail. One evening, hours after the fighting had stopped and all seemed quiet, he began to scout the trail to prepare for the next day's skirmish. Suddenly, a shot came out of nowhere. In an instant, he was gone. No one knew which side shot him; to this day, it remains an unanswered question for his family. As the war worsened, his wife and daughters struggled to feed themselves and survive on their own. Many men were killed—uncles, fathers, husbands, and brothers—and it was a harrowing time for many families. Fortunately, Malia's mother had taught her daughters to weave, passing down the skill she learned

homes. A lot of the pricing models for things were driven by the cost as opposed to the value. "But the model that we're seeing today is very new. Companies are getting smart and creating an ecosystem," Gansky explains. "You build systems and services that make sense for a particular opportunity."

This is what I had in mind when I started Lulan Artisans. One day in 2003, I was research-ing textiles in Gensler's materials library in San Francisco. I told the librarian about my company and its mission. He later walked over and quietly handed me a business card. I looked down at the card and saw only a name, a phone number, and a title. "Call her," he said. "She's a textile designer. You will want to work with her. She will understand exactly what you want to do." So I did, and she invited me to her home later that week. I was just starting out. All I had was a vision and a name for the company. Yet as I told her about the weavers and my ideas, her whole face lit up. She wanted to get involved.

That woman was Laura Guido-Clark, a world-class textile designer and colorist who has worked for companies such as Apple, Frog Design, Design Within Reach, Interface FLOR—and now, Lulan. She and another extremely talented textile designer, Michael Koch, were intimately involved with the creation of our first two collections, 11/17 and Organic Symmetry. For each piece in a collection, we create a computer drawing and from her own mother. Weaving helped them survive, because they could trade textiles for food.

Though the war ended more than thirty years ago, Malia told this story as if it happened yesterday. I had known Malia for years. I had met her whole family. As her business partner and longtime friend, I realized that my being American was now only a small part of who I was to her. But I wondered what she must have felt when she first met me. I felt a weight on my shoulders—a responsibility—because I was American. We both cried as she continued her story. I apologized, and we sat together, our arms locked. The love of weaving and craftsmanship had brought us together and, without our realizing it, that love had stripped away the cultural identities that we sometimes inadvertently wear. We were now clothed in a new garment of simple human compassion. We were two women—sharing life's joys, sorrows, past stories, and similar hopes and dreams, connected more deeply than we had ever imagined.

DISRUPTIVE ENTREPRENEUR
TOBIAS ROSE-STOCKWELL / HUMAN TRANSLATION

Tobias Rose-Stockwell is the founder of the nonprofit Human Translation, which builds sustainable solutions to poverty by helping communities help themselves.

initial color scheme. The artisans use this drawing to make a weave sample. If necessary for technical guidance, we also provide what's called a weave draft drawing, which depicts the pattern on graph paper. We deliberately don't overexplain the designs, because we want the master artisans to interpret them for themselves. This is where the magic begins. Receiving a finished sample is often a delightful surprise, usually better than we expected. In rare cases where something gets lost in translation, we discard those designs. It's worth it to have a few that don't work in exchange for maintaining a looseness in the process that keeps everyone involved. From concept to designer to final product, everyone adds his or her expertise along the way. Laura and Michael's contribution remains palpable, because it's part of a layering effect, enriching the work of all Lulan's collaborators.

In building Lulan, I learned that the interconnection of people's activities creates an energy greater than whatever brought those people together—in our case, our company or our container of collaboration. It's not just about the founder or the products or the people; it's about all that is possible. When your company structure allows for this, you create the opportunity for surprising contributions that can have significant results for your business. The right container for collaboration takes on a life of its own: It draws people in, those people spark new ideas, and their ideas and aspirations become

The power of circumstance is what really motivated me to participate in social change. I studied studio arts at Allegheny College in Pennsylvania, and in 2003, a few years after graduating, I traveled to Thailand for volunteer work. I worked at an orphanage for HIV-positive children in Nong Khai, in the northeast. Even though I was completely out of my comfort zone, I felt this powerful connection to the children and saw the positive impact my time with them had on their lives. I decided to extend my trip and visit Cambodia. As I traveled there, I was regularly amazed by the stories of survival that I heard. It seemed that anyone over the age of thirty-five knew someone who was killed, went insane, or was involved in the fighting during the Khmer Rouge years.

One day, a monk invited me to his home in the countryside. When we got there, several hundred villagers were waiting. They told me they had a problem with their reservoir, which was the primary source of irrigation for rice fields that fed about 9,000 people. The reservoir also provided protein for the villagers because it doubled as a fishery. This important source of irrigation and food had been there for 1,000 years, but it had been severely damaged by the Khmer Rouge to the point where it was nonfunctional. The villagers wanted my help. I told them they had the wrong person—I didn't know anything about irrigation and reservoirs—but they persisted. I said I'd talk with others, and soon, I found myself pulled into this project because I had a great connection

part of the overall self-enriching cycle. I have discovered several important steps for forming viable, valuable business partnerships:

Listen

Intrepid entrepreneur Paul Polak—whose masterful book, *Out of Poverty*, offers a grassroots blueprint for poverty eradication in developing countries—describes the challenge of bringing ventures to new areas: "Done right, the concept of outsider doesn't exist. In essence, people in every village in every country are open to innovation. They don't care where it comes from. But the implementation has to be local and culturally relevant. If not, you will fail."

This perspective is crucial to building strong collaborations. The first thing I do when I arrive at a new weaving cooperative is listen. I want to know how the cooperative is organized, socially and structurally, and the extent of its capabilities. Does the region consistently supply the necessary raw materials? Does the cooperative raise its own silkworms or buy silk from other groups? Do the artists use other natural fibers, such as organic cotton, linen, and wool? Are there thirty artisans or 200? Does the cooperative have diverse enough skills to produce a variety of designs? Do the craftspeople dye their own yarn or fabric? What is their work philosophy? Does with the community. I realized something simple and powerful: I could help in some way and make a difference.

I ended up going back and forth to Cambodia to get more information about the project and to meet with the officials in charge of water resources. I also set up a partnership with the volunteer organization Engineers Without Borders. We looked at soil quality and the structure's history. Just before the engineers started work, we discovered that there were landmines all over, so we couldn't do anything until the mines were cleared. We quickly realized that if we just came in and rebuilt the reservoir, the whole process wouldn't work. There needed to be true community engagement. If the community didn't want this project, it wasn't going to be successful. I learned that a major part of the process was expectation management. They needed to have a realistic sense of what we could deliver and when. We calibrated their wants, not just needs, to reach the best possible outcome for them.

We also said we wouldn't do this project unless a couple of things happened. We needed local labor, materials, and financial support. All of us agreed that we would have to put our hearts and souls into this project for it to be successful. So the villagers committed what they could, which was donated materials and labor.

the cooperative treat all artisans well? Is the workshop comfortable, with cross ventilation and shade? Does it consider the needs of the artisans' families and the wider community? What are the desires, goals, and dreams of the members for their cooperative? Together, how can we organize to reach those goals? Listening is vital for understanding how to build the right collaborations.

Structure business around culture

A room of weavers is not just a workshop. It's part of a larger community structure. Some weavers, for instance, are primarily rice farmers. Part of the year they produce textiles, the rest they spend harvesting and planting. For some, weaving and artisanal work is supplemental; their real economic opportunities lie elsewhere. For others, weaving is their primary vocation.

Lulan works with cooperatives that have structured themselves as full-time weaving centers. But even these dedicated weavers take two weeks every year to help their extended families with the rice crop. Weaving in these communities has always been organized around seasonal activities. There is a rhythm to life in Southeast Asia, and it touches everything in the workshops, including the fabrics produced. For example, humidity affects the color of dyes, so that a blue produced in the rainy season is

If you're from a developed country, people in less developed nations sometimes assume you bring lots of money, and they target you to make money. These kinds of expectations can make the whole project more expensive. But because we were all volunteering together, we were seen as a cohesive team, which was very helpful. We were all there for the same reasons. Early on, we estimated that it would take about $20,000 to rebuild the reservoir—and we were really far off. Later, a development bank scoped the project and said it would cost $3.5 million. Ultimately, we did it for $300,000. We could never have done it for that amount if the community hadn't contributed time and about $15,000 worth of local materials.

Now, with funding from the United Nations Development Programme, we have expanded our model and reach. We help farmers in Cambodia through the installation of major irrigation systems and low-cost filters, improving yields by up to 300 percent. We also help set up household fishponds for villagers. This allows farmers and villagers to provide food for their families. The people of these villages have been through tremendous hardship. And we come from different parts of the world—there are language barriers, cultural barriers, and economic barriers. There are many walls that we have to get over, but we work together and accomplish something special, changing things for the better.

different from a blue produced in the dry season. Part of the dyers' crucial expertise is understanding these fluctuations and accounting for them in the production of fabrics consistent with Lulan's color standards. It's part of the Lulan philosophy to create a high-quality product through the integration of nature and skill, rather than relying on industrialized methods that are harmful ecologically.

With talents cultivated through generations, these master artisans are unique in the larger global marketplace. Yet this highly skilled labor force remains largely untapped. Many people in Southeast Asia are being trained by international organizations and NGOs in new farming techniques or computer skills so they can work full time in those industries. Weavers continue practicing a craft for which they already are trained, and exquisitely so. A diverse labor force in every country is important, for sure. But it is crucial to design for skills and talents already in place. Doing so brings real value, culturally and systemically. It makes new ventures feasible for and appealing to local communities and, ultimately, makes success possible.

Build the company around people

Rather than impose our methods, we work with what exists on the ground. If a weaving community has certain skills, Lulan creates appropriate products for those skills and finds the right market for them through our sales channels. We don't try to fundamentally change things. We build on what the artisans already know by learning from them and including them in the process. Gansky says it well: "An effective Mesh is sort of like tofu—it takes on the flavor of whom and what is around it." By building the company around the people, you soak up that flavor.

Make meaningful products

A growing number of customers is seeking out high-quality workmanship instead of cookie-cutter design. There is an increasing desire for handmade products. The popularity of magazines such as *Make* and *Hand/Eye* testifies to the rising interest in artisanal products, as does the success of the Web site Etsy, an online artisanal marketplace that directly connects creators to buyers. The arts-and-crafts movement is once again an established market, and Lulan products are at the heart of this resurgence.

We combine high style with integrated sustainable and social attributes. By respecting the work of the artisans, we produce meaningful products that customers want. We make fabrics with rich, unusual colors that, while hand dyed, still meet the consistency standards of the demanding interior design market. "I recently used a silk of an indescribable color," says well-known Charleston interior designer Amelia T. Handegan, a Lulan customer. "It had maybe three colors woven into a solid, which created a very diverse iridescent fabric....It changed from coral to orange to pink!" At the same time, some seeming imperfections in the weaving enhance the beauty of the handcrafted fabric. Our artisans know the difference between a problem and a naturally occurring variation that becomes part of the art form. This commitment to a level of quality embedded in the production process is part of the story of our products.

Bring value

By collaborating with men and women in the community, we're showing that we care about them and value their cultural techniques and skills. We also want to assure them that we're in this for the long haul. We'd like to help train new generations of weavers and artisans, and help create the next design sprouts. We try to show the artisans that, with some technical training, minor adjustments to their methods, and basic business education, they can take their products into new markets. We work with them on skills they can use for the rest of their lives. There is great joy in working with these communities. We believe that honest collaboration is the highest form of respect and appreciation.

Embrace community as your partner

Every time we make decisions about our products, we "show and tell" the artisans why. As our partners, they need to know the desires of the buyers and what will sell in different markets. They also have to be part of problem solving so they can more easily exercise their skills, experience, and ingenuity to the benefit of our business. For example, market research may indicate that light blue is "out" one season and deeper blues are "in." Or the weavers may be producing one kind of design, and we need another. Lulan involves the artisans in making these shifts. These master craftspeople may not know the latest trends, but they know something more important: the sophisticated technical processes behind the products. New designs or colors don't always work. But even a failed experiment helps the artisans increase their savvy about the international marketplace. Together, we merge new ideas with incredible expertise. The results of this powerful combination become part of the larger community, taught to others within the cooperative or to weavers in the next village or town.

Polak recalls his initial efforts to get a treadle pump to villagers. This foot-powered device, designed to lift water from as deep as 23 feet, can do most of the work of a motorized pump but costs considerably less. "Early on, we focused a lot of time on building a killer technology, but we soon realized that we'd need to spend most of our time solving the last-mile distribution problem; that is, actually getting the pump into the hands of the people who need it. Today we spend 75 percent of our time, effort, and money on the distribution of the technology, rather than building the technology itself. So the key is to create a profitable last-mile supply chain, and that always entails getting the community actively involved."

Incubate your future partners

As the weaving cooperatives become well versed in business and design, they begin to see ways to create their own spin-off enterprises, which, in turn, become exactly the kind of groups Lulan wants to partner with. In this way, Lulan can serve as a business incubator—a powerful future model for our company. These tangential ventures are examples of design sprouts. And the more we can encourage and assist the next generation of entrepreneurs in these countries, the more design sprouts abound.

For years, Lulan has worked with Nhean, a thriving entrepreneur from Cambodia with his own weaving center. An expert dyer, he built the workshop and hired the spinners, dyers, weavers, and finishers. While working with a variety of international clients, he started having trouble managing everything by himself. His primary problem was cash flow. Nhean had borrowed money from his family and in-laws to start the business. But any profits were going back into running the shop, and Nhean was feeling the pressure of his responsibilities. How was he going to pay off the original investment and expand his enterprise? He asked Lulan to take over the weaving center. We did so, on the condition that he stay on to help manage the center and learn new business skills.

We wanted to bolster Nhean so he could become a partner with us in the weaving center. But what wound up happening was even better. While still working part-time at the center, Nhean started two other successful businesses: dyeing for different weaving groups and being the exclusive distributor for a low-impact dye company. Both ventures highlight his strengths yet are manageable for him, and he enjoys being involved in the weaving center without carrying the day-to-day stress alone. Lulan has since begun working with Nhean through both of his new businesses.

The story of our collaboration with Nhean demonstrates a key element of systems thinking: understanding the roles and interests of stakeholders, the people who represent every aspect of a project or problem—economic, ecological, social, cultural, communal, and personal. The range of stakeholders in a business includes employees, distributors, wholesalers, retailers, suppliers, partners, creditors, stockholders, communities, governments (city, state, federal, and international), NGOs, competitors, and the general public. It's important to have teamwork among all levels. Usually, the most important stakeholder is the customer. But in creating Lulan, I focused equally on artisans and buyers, because we need to understand both. That means listening carefully, and listening means market and customer research. Nathan Shedroff, chair of the groundbreaking MBA in Design Strategy at California College of the Arts in San Francisco, has a great definition of marketing in regards to systems thinking in design and business. "Marketing," he says, "is the inhale. It's what you learn from your customers, producers, markets, competitors, and industries. Sales are the exhale—the messaging you put together and communicate in order to talk to your customers, producers, markets, competitors, and industries. Too few companies understand this, and, as a result, most aren't inhaling well—or at all."

This concept of inhale/exhale is appropriately systemic. I've had to learn to inhale a lot in building Lulan, and I started long before I even conceived of this as a business. When I first came to Vietnam and found the weavers, I inhaled all I could about their processes, techniques, needs, and goals. When I talk to potential design-industry customers, I inhale what they see in the market, what their clients are telling them and buying, what challenges exist in the supply chain. I do the same when I speak with interior designers, retailers, and other customers. By structuring your business as a container for collaboration, you build in this inhaling and exhaling. It brings you new ideas, new sources of inspiration, and new products to offer the marketplace.

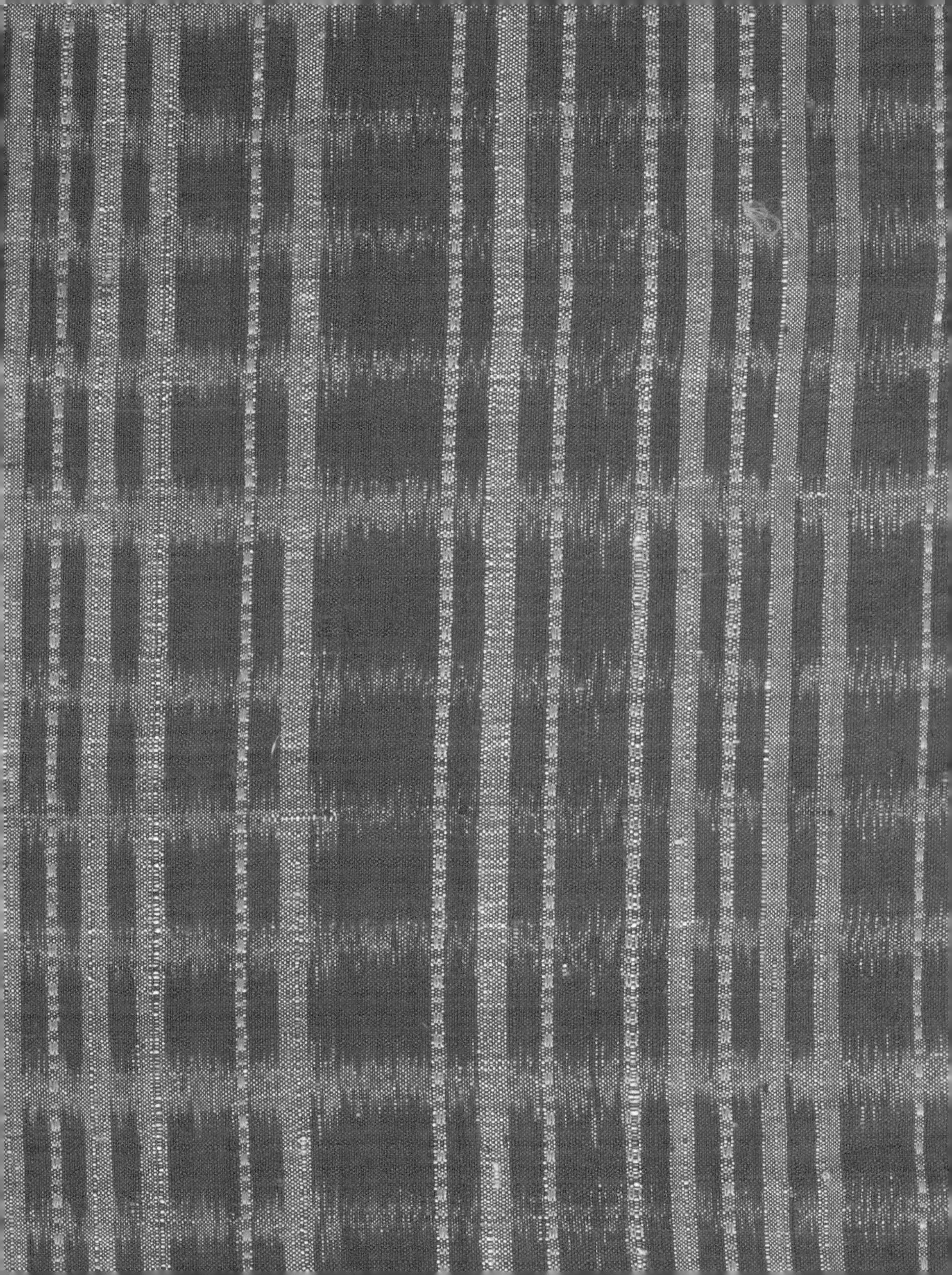

SUSTAINABILITY IN 6-D

WEAVING KNOWLEDGE INTO CHANGE

I decided to expand Lulan Artisans' business beyond Southeast Asia to India. It was an easy decision, because I was interested in making a difference in this vast and culturally complex country, while also diversifying our craftsmanship and tapping India's rich supply of natural fibers, including organic cotton, wool, linen, and silk. Before we began working in India, Lulan was producing only silk and cotton products. This would give us access to new fibers. The incredible Indian artists I had met on my visits to the country also had the skills and drive to be a productive and great addition to our team.

India is experiencing dramatic changes as a rising financial power. It also faces significant challenges in terms of human trafficking, poverty, gender equality, and education. During this time of India's fast-paced development, I wanted to help the many artisans who exist outside the mainstream economic changes.

As I planned for the Indian expansion, I sought to create additional containers for collaboration by having a local partner. Usually, a manager at one of the weaving cooperatives serves as Lulan's key contact for that group. But for India, Lulan needed more general oversight, because the country is so vast and diverse. I chose two people, a man and a woman, to manage the many different artisan groups across regions, cultures, and

THE PRACTICAL PATH TO SUSTAINABILITY:
A CHECKLIST FOR ACTION

Lulan Artisans began from a simple idea: to integrate gorgeous designs into beautiful woven fabrics that would appeal to an international market. But there was a larger vision as well, which was to create a for-profit social venture that improves the lives and communities of artisans. Our work brought us into direct, close contact with remarkable people whose creativity, resourcefulness, and stories are expressed in their unique artworks.

The products that our artisan partners create come out of a deep and time-honored tradition, practiced in weaving communities in villages, towns, and cities. Their devotion to the craft goes back generations. An important factor for Lulan is to not only sustain but also improve their professional and personal lives by providing an adequate income. These people are not just workers. They are mothers and fathers, sons and daughters. They are artists. They are community leaders. All are inheritors of a rich cultural legacy, which they—and we—want to sustain for future generations.

"Sustainability" is one of those buzzwords we hear a lot these days. Often, it's shorthand for business practices that have no negative impact on the global or local ecology, languages. Lulan collaborates with artisans practicing traditions from embroidery to woodblock printing, in workshops located everywhere from the mountainous state of Nagaland to the cosmopolitan city of Jaipur. Some of our artisans speak Hindi, India's principal official language. Others belong to tribal groups that speak some of the country's several hundred different dialects.

Early in the process of connecting with Indian partners, the woman I was working with, Rashmi, said: "Tell me in detail the intent behind Lulan Artisans." I explained how we worked from the ground up, and how the needs and futures of artisan communities play a deep role in our collaborations. After listening, she said that most companies she had worked with did not have this philosophy or approach—or, if they did, they did not share this information with her. We discussed how important this transfer of knowledge is to really make systemic change.

On my next trip to India, Rashmi and I spent long days working together. During that time, she revealed that Lulan had inspired her in several ways. She told me she had found an artisan family to assist, and that she was working hard to get their products, such as scarves, shawls, and pillows, into the marketplace. This was wonderful.

society, or economy. A "sustainable" business strives to meet the triple bottom line of planet, people, and profit. But there are a few essential elements missing from these considerations. Organizations of all types are reviewing and revamping supply chains— their sourcing, manufacturing, distribution, and outsourcing processes—and this is a great start. Too often, though, our businesses extract a hidden cultural cost. By overlaying our needs on those of other countries and value systems, we can break down, weaken, and even eradicate tightly woven cultural supports.

If diversity is important to ecologies and makes markets, systems, and societies more resilient, then there is little doubt that cultures, too, should be diverse, in order to represent our collective learning and perspectives. Unfortunately, indigenous cultures are depleted, like other natural resources, when well-meaning organizations seek to "lift" local communities to their own standards. If we truly want a 360-degree view of sustainability, why stop at ecological, social, and financial considerations? Yes, let's look at the input and output of materials, resources, and capital. But let's also look at culturally relevant impacts and business models. This is "cultural sustainability."

Lulan was born of a business model that tries at a very fundamental level to understand both its customers and its employees. We consciously celebrate the uniqueness of

Months passed, and on my next visit Rashmi mentioned that she and her husband were ready to start a family. They were having difficulties conceiving, and we discussed the idea of adoption. In India, historically, adoption is uncommon for reasons having to do with the caste system. Acceptance is growing, although baby girls are more frequently available. Also, girls are often seen as second-class citizens or burdens to their families because of dowry practices and cultural prejudices that prevent women from working. According to a UNICEF report, 7,000 fewer girls are born daily in India compared to global averages, because many Indian women seek abortions when they learn a fetus is female. Some parents kill girl babies right after birth. The Indian government estimates that at least 10 million female fetuses or babies have been aborted or killed in the past twenty years. With this in mind, Rashmi and her husband adopted a baby girl.

One night, while we worked over Skype, Rashmi told me she was going to start her own business. She wanted to work with clients in a new way, representing artisans with an approach modeled on ours at Lulan. My journey, which began with one company, one container of collaboration, was expanding beautifully through others—through design sprouts. I had wanted to create something that would inspire people into action, and here, with Rashmi, that came to pass.

the different cultures where our products originate. Our focus goes beyond providing safe, well-ventilated working conditions and fair wages. It includes using traditional processes and natural materials that have worked for centuries. We honor the expertise that gives these societies a competitive advantage—expertise such as knowing how to weave ikats and brocades. This isn't something universal; there aren't groups of people in every country in the world with these abilities. The preservation of these specialized skills is an imperative for these cultures—and, by extension, for Lulan. Our artisans want to make inroads into the global marketplace without renouncing their cultural identities. Lulan's collaborative business model respects the artisans' integrity. This kind of inclusivity can have a huge impact on productivity and resiliency for entire communities in the developing world.

In the process of designing Lulan, I had to consider the physical practicalities involved in turning visions into realities. The company needed to achieve sustainability on six different levels: ecological, social, economic, communal, personal, and cultural.

Ecological: Big feet, small footprints

By now, we are quite familiar with the dire need for ecological sustainability. Increasing threats of pollution, resource depletion, and climate change have pushed our

DISRUPTIVE ENTREPRENEUR
MUNA ABUSULAYMAN / *KALAM NAWAEM*

Muna AbuSulayman is one of the Arab world's leading media personalities. She is a founding co-host of the all-female talk show Kalam Nawaem, *one of the most popular social programs on the pan-Arab satellite network MBC. As the secretary-general of the Alwaleed Bin Talal Kingdom Foundation (AFTB), she overseas global humanitarian and philanthropic projects in areas including poverty alleviation, disaster relief, and the empowerment of women. In 2005, she became the first woman in Saudi Arabia to be appointed by the United Nations Development Programme as a goodwill ambassador.*

I deal with bureaucracy a lot, and every single day I have to go up against many intractable forces, whether they're Middle Eastern cultural institutions or Western prejudices and preconceptions. But what always gets me excited in the morning, even as I have to face these challenges on a daily basis, is that I know the work I do matters. I get the opportunity to meet people who tell wonderful stories, and that gives me strength. Our show covers many different topics, including women's issues. We focus on what is really at the root of a problem and explore that fully. Many women in our culture simply don't have the right to make their own choices. So a show can, ostensibly, be on a specific topic, but it really is about changing the paradigm of our culture and empowering women.

natural resources to the brink. In just the last century, humanity has destroyed half its wetlands and forests and nearly three-quarters of its marine fisheries, according to the Worldwatch Institute. The modern-day textile industry is one of the world's biggest polluters, from the pesticides used to grow cotton, to the immense amount of energy it takes to produce synthetics, to the toxic dyes that contaminate watersheds. Ecological sustainability is especially crucial in the developing world, where many countries are primarily agrarian. Yet, in some cases, a reliance on subsistence agriculture for survival has taxed already degraded watersheds and depleted biodiversity. Artisanal weavers prove an exception here, because their traditional processes are more ecologically responsible. Lulan uses all-natural materials, such as silk, organic cotton, wool, and linen, as well as natural or low-impact dyes. Natural fibers are healthier for the environment, and the fact that these cooperatives had already been using organic materials for centuries fits with the Lulan philosophy of building the business around the culture.

The natural dyes we use vary from country to country, depending on the available flowers, fruits, plants, or, in some cases, insects. To produce beautiful reds, pinks, and purples, some dyers in Southeast Asia rely on beetles that secrete a scarlet resin called lac onto tree branches. The hardened lac can be collected, crushed, and used to make

There is a reason our show is extremely successful: We openly discuss important issues that, before, nobody talked about. These are often subjects relating to huge taboos in my culture, whether it's my divorce and how I'm dealing with it, or child abuse, or incest. These things were just not discussed. But we really need to talk about these issues openly as a society and as a culture in order to grow and thrive. We have done shows, for instance, about honor killing, which is the murder of someone by family or clan members who believe the victim has brought dishonor upon the family or community. But instead of attacking the government about what they should be doing to stop this practice, we openly discuss it. We get a conversation going and we make sure the issues are presented in a way that the debate is constructive.

Often, in my world, you see a lot of young girls who think their futures are limited and that they cannot attain great things. I want them to think differently. I want them to realize that there is so much more to the world than what they have experienced or thought possible. There is a vast world of opportunity beyond their perceived parameters.

Each year on our show, we choose a topic to champion. One year it was literacy, particularly among women. This is a very big problem in many parts of the world. In the Arab culture, we have a huge number of women in their thirties who are considered

not only dye but also varnish. The terms "shellac" and "lacquer" originated with this process. Other natural dye sources include ebony fruit for gray and black, wild almond for golden brown, annatto seed for orange, and indigo mixed with other plants for green.

The weavers recycle and conserve as much as possible during manufacturing: they collect rainwater, burn rice husks to boil water for dyes, and reuse the dye baths. Although not a standard practice, reusing a dye bath means, for example, that a deep red will become a light red and, finally, a pink. Such simple measures have reduced the average water usage in our cooperatives easily by half. For many people, such ecological frugality is simply part of living in a country with limited resources. Our weavers utilize time-honored processes to make quantities of fabric and products their ancestors never dreamed of. This commitment to the local ecology is part of the value of this process.

Social: Assistance, not dependence

Lulan's relationship with independent cooperatives is a true partnership, built on assistance and not dependence. As with any partner, we seek a symbiotic relationship. "Business relationships must be seen as a conversation, and the various stakeholders illiterate. Some cannot read at all; others struggle with reading comprehension. So we brought in women who were accomplished college graduates—some of them famous. We had them join us with their mothers, who were illiterate. Then we had the women interview their moms. One of the most powerful interviews was a doctor who told her mother, "I just want you to be able to read labels on medicine and dangerous items so you will not harm yourself." And it was so powerful, because that's not the usual way we think about literacy. We think about literacy for knowledge, yet here was a woman who was almost crying. It's not about knowledge. It's not about religion. It's about keeping people safe. Moments like that really count.

In a larger sense, I really want the media all over the world to change. I want the obsessive drive for ratings to stop and, instead, for media to cover important issues that matter to our culture. That's how our culture grows and thrives. I envision media as not beholden to any group or government agency but looking out for the needs of citizens and consumers. I want human rights to be the No. 1 issue we cover as journalists. It's our most important concern, throughout the world—how we treat each other and how this can be improved.

//

must not be afraid to participate," says Nathan Shedroff. But, he admits, this new form of business is not always easy.

Lulan's integrated business model creates opportunities for farmers, spinners, dyers, weavers, and finishers—men and women—and inspires other cooperatives to do the same. Most of our cooperatives handle every step in the process of creating their textiles. A cooperative that works with silk, for instance, will include farmers nearby with mulberry trees and silkworm eggs. Once hatched, the worms eat mulberry leaves until they make cocoons. The cocoons are then boiled to remove the sericin, the sticky protein that binds the silk threads. Spinners twist the threads together to make a stronger strand. They next combine the silk into a skein—a length of many threads wound on a reel—and boil it again to degum it of any leftover sericin. The silk is then washed, dyed, dried in the sun, and spun in preparation for the loom. A warper— usually a manager or weaver—takes some of the threads and creates the warp, the set of lengthwise yarns held in tension on the weaving frame or loom. Setting up the warp can take as long as three days. When the warp is ready, the weaver starts inserting the weft yarn over and under the warp, creating a piece of fabric. Finishers wash the fabric; they also make fringe at the end if the final product is a scarf, shawl, or throw. Sewers complete other products such as pillows, duvets, or wallets.

The government services and social safety nets that many developed countries take for granted do not exist here. Instead, villagers and townspeople depend solely on communal support systems. What Lulan does is support the artisans' cooperative working methods by offering quality-of-life benefits. For example, we pay for numerous costs associated with the education of the artisans' children, including their annual school fees and the uniforms they wear each day to class.

At one of the cooperatives in Cambodia, we have a talented manager and head warper named Sop. When we began working with this cooperative, the country manager and I discussed our policy of educating the artisans' children when they reach school age. Lulan provides that benefit for all children—girls and boys. It doesn't matter if they have already missed some years of school; they are enrolled at the level that makes sense for them.

Sop had been working with Lulan for two years when she finally approached the country manager. She explained that she had an adopted eight-year-old daughter and asked if Lulan would consider her the same as the other children and assist with her education. When the manager shared this exchange with me, I was crushed. Of course we would educate her daughter like the others! This child had lost two years of schooling, so we enrolled her immediately. Whenever an artisan joins a weaving center, we describe our education policy; but in this case, Sop assumed her daughter was ineligible because she was adopted. This wasn't just a communication breakdown; it was also a cultural breakdown.

Lulan allows each artisan group to choose benefits tailored to its particular needs. Beyond support for their children's education, other benefits can include literacy classes, day care, healthcare, or monthly housing stipends. Lulan also promotes a healthy, safe, and sustainable working environment for the weavers. The cooperative sets its own work schedule to accommodate household, family, and agricultural needs. In addition, we do not use child labor. All of our workers are at least eighteen. Most of the weavers we work with place a strong emphasis on educating their children. If family life is stable and productive, we see clear benefits throughout the community. That is true social sustainability—in any country.

Economic: Growing together

A simple but important question must guide economic decisions: Does the relationship work for all parties involved? This is part of systems thinking. Shedroff notes, "It's essential that all parts be interconnected, so that if one group benefits, everyone benefits."

Lulan Artisans begins by partnering with cooperatives that are already operational. The communities need to have demonstrated the ambition and energy to establish a manufacturing structure to produce and sell their products. Lulan can best help them design and sell their wares by working within their current setup. Then, together, we can modify certain aspects in order to make them more successful.

As part of our goal to bring value to the community, we assist with design, business, marketing, and distribution. But our partners must have an awareness of the possibilities for their businesses, and they need to decide, purposefully, that they want to tackle specific challenges to better succeed in the marketplace. We aren't in a position to create this drive, only to nurture it. Economic sustainability grows by connecting the workshops with a diversified market and thereby generating long-term financial opportunities.

Communal: Vital, sustained connection

The definition of "community" has evolved over time. It used to mean, quite simply, a group of people with a common life. Soon, community became shorthand for a village or town. In the wired world of today, a community knows no such constraints on location. Vibrant online communities are often defined by shared affinities, whether it's a love of rock climbing or jazz. Individuals may not see their fellow community members, but the connection is alive. Interestingly, some people within virtual communities, such as Facebook and Twitter, still want to meet face-to-face, hence the development of tweetups. It seems there's still something very satisfying in the physical aspect of a community.

As modernization continues, we move more and travel more. This changes the way our communities are created—or, in some cases, radically transformed. For example, the pull of job opportunities in cities worldwide has dramatically disassembled centuries-old agricultural communities. Also, as people move from one city to another more easily, communities start to feel transient. Yet, despite these changes, communities—in whatever form they take—continue to play a foundational role in our lives. The nurturing of communities is a critical part of Lulan's business model. Strength and support, we believe, come from the community. Beauty and life come from the community. Our communities—our artisans, our sellers, our customers—may be separated by great physical distances, but we bring them together purposefully and respectfully.

Personal: Inclusive well-being

Sustainability is not just an ecological, social, economic, communal, or cultural concern; it's also a personal value. Just as we need to maintain the vitality of a town or village, we need to sustain our energy, emotion, spirit, and finances as well as our mental and physical health. We can see this clearly in our relationships as well as our emotional well-being. Most important, we all need sustainable love. Sustainable emotional relationships are the foundation for sustainable cultural relationships. They create productive communities and economic stability. They become a part of us fundamentally.

Just as we need systems thinking in regards to design and business, so we need to rethink our relationships. Our social structures and gender roles are shifting radically. Applying the old models no longer works, but we haven't even begun the conversations about, let alone the redesign of, these systems. And if we are going to have a truly sustainable society—or, better yet, a thriving one—we must nurture the emotional well-being in our lives. Most fathers and mothers love their children, yet—as I saw firsthand in Hanoi—some parents in desperate economic situations will sell their children for sex or forced labor in order to sustain the rest of the family. Improved economic opportunities increase the chances that love and connection will be maintained.

We say all the time how passionate entrepreneurs are about their ideas. But while we're comfortable speaking about passion in business, we also need to be comfortable including compassion in business. We talk about respecting the earth and one another, but the word "respect" can allow some distance. We need to love the earth and love one another. Love and business can be combined with successful models that are profitable and honor our humanity. I saw up close the efficient, savvy, profitable business of human trafficking—a business devoid of any compassion or love. We can only win this struggle if we are just as determined and savvy in our own businesses, and if we have the additional strength of love and compassion on our side.

As the global economy powers on, humanity continues to devour large amounts of food, entertainment, products, and services. People want the latest smartphone, electronic gadget, or car, throwing away the old models almost as soon as new models are available. We are, unfortunately, a throwaway culture. These obsessions are not solely U.S.-centric but have permeated many places. What happens when we treat our relationships the same way—as throwaways? But our proclivities toward creating a cast-off society are neither inevitable nor irreversible. Moment by moment, we make choices that determine our values and direction. If we base decisions on love, rather than consumption, a new world of personal and economic growth awaits.

Cultural: A philosophy of cooperation

Culture affects every social, economic, and ecological decision a community makes. Sensitivity to customs, language, rituals, aspirations, and acceptable forms of innovation is a prerequisite for the formation of mutually enhancing businesses that are integral to communities. In the high-tech world there is much talk about "technology transfer"—the process of sharing skills, knowledge, and technologies among groups to ensure that developments are accessible to a wider range of individuals. Lulan promotes its own version of "technology transfer," whereby ideas from everyone involved flow throughout and infiltrate the entire organization. This exchange makes our business more solid. For example, one community may handle its weaving and pattern creation very differently from another, in ways that save time and energy. It is important that each group be willing to share its best practices with other artisan centers, allowing people to learn things they never would outside of this partnership. Our take on technology transfer is at the very heart of the philosophy of collaboration.

One night I got an e-mail from a weaver. "Hey," she wrote. "We went to a village and they were setting up some looms the same, novel way Lulan does." She was referring to how we prepare looms and buy materials ahead of time in anticipation of incoming orders. I was intrigued. "How did they learn that?" I asked. "They said the village that taught them this was working with an international company called Lulan." Peer-to-peer sharing—that's the strength of our model.

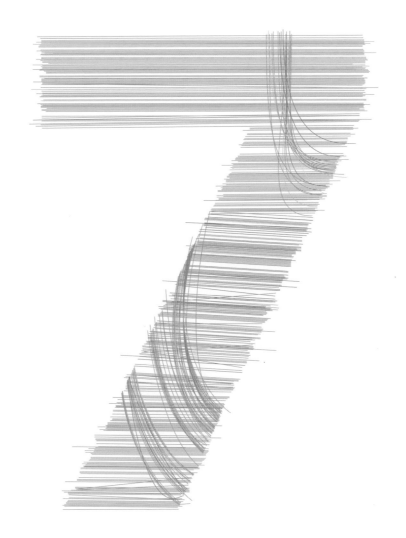

THE POWER OF STORY

COMING HOME

By 1975, many Laotians had fled their country. Decades of war had scarred the land and its people, and many citizens sought to begin life anew in Europe and the United States. Two Laotian expats, Alana and Noi, met after they had relocated to France and were attending college. They fell in love and married. Over the years that the couple lived in the south of France, the world began to slowly but inexorably change. The cold war abated, and separations that had existed for generations between countries and cultures started to fall away.

The displaced Laotians longed for home. Noi was an environmental research scientist, and Alana had a great eye for design and craft. They felt they could apply their talents back in their native country, because the economic markets of Southeast Asia were starting to open up. More deeply, they wanted to use their skills to aid their homeland.

In the early 1990s, they returned to Laos. Economically, the country was slowly on the rise, and there was new business activity. Flush with entrepreneurial spirit, Alana started a nonprofit weaving center built on sustainable business practices. She used fibers grown without harmful or destructive chemicals and colored with natural, nonpolluting dyes. In addition to her business, she became involved in governmental

A COMMON THREAD

Throughout our whole lives, we are surrounded by stories. Stories help us make sense of confusion and chaos. They organize our varied experiences into a common thread and unite us. We all laugh. We all cry. We all bubble over with joy or collapse with grief. We all struggle. Most elementally, stories link us emotionally to other human beings who share our aspirations and challenges. "That is the beauty of the narrative," says Joe Lambert, executive director of the Center for Digital Storytelling, a nonprofit that assists people in using digital media to tell meaningful stories from their lives. "There's a little handshake here with a person you may not have ever met, which says, 'I know what you're going through. It creates a very real emotional connection.'"

We continually tell each other stories about every aspect of our lives: of success or failure, of power or vulnerability. Some stories endure for a day, others for a month or even a lifetime. We have stories about our work, about our families and relationships, about what we hope for and what we're capable of achieving. Telling stories provides structure and direction as we navigate life's challenges and opportunities. Stories profoundly affect how others see us and we see ourselves. "The best stories start with fact and they rapidly move into our imagination," notes artist Brian Andreas of StoryPeople, an online forum for storytelling and marketplace for art, crafts, and

and handicraft organizations to help nurture and sustain the craft industry. Lulan collaborates with Alana, working on some of Lulan's line of home furnishings and accessories.

Alana and Noi are not alone. Many expatriates from Southeast Asia have returned to their native countries after fleeing the terrible conflicts that ripped the region apart from the 1950s through the 1980s. Many moved back after starting families overseas, and they want their children to understand their heritage and culture. They feel a desire to help their birth countries and, for the first time, they see an opening. These are the disruptive entrepreneurs who practice "boomerang change." After learning skills abroad, they return home and use their talents to make large and positive impacts. In doing so, they connect their two worlds—their identities as sophisticated innovators and passionate citizens.

DISRUPTIVE ENTREPRENEUR
TALI GOTTLIEB / ISRAEL PHILHARMONIC ORCHESTRA FOUNDATION

As executive director of the Israel Philharmonic Orchestra Foundation, Tali Gottlieb helps carry on the vision of a Polish violinist who saw a way to use music to promote understanding, collaboration, and peace across a broad range of cultural and religious

other products. "We use stories as a way to create a world in which people want to be part of something meaningful, where they feel connected."

Stories can also create solidarity and spark dramatic change, especially if they allow us to see the world with fresh eyes. In 1954, when the Algerians rose up against the French colonial government at the beginning of an eight-year war of independence, officials began to systematically arrest Algerian storytellers, fearing their tales were fanning unified resistance to French rule. At that time, illiteracy was high among Algerians, so traditional stories were passed along orally. By tweaking and updating these ancient tales—the French were cast as evil, while the Algerians were heroic patriots—the storytellers became threateningly subversive. This episode in history demonstrates how stories evolve—casting new characters in age-old plots—and how each new generation of a story can teach powerful lessons about universal themes, from love and hate to conflict and triumph. Even in our digital age, we've seen iconic tales play out in narratives in Silicon Valley: how a garage startup became Apple, or how college friends founded eBay or PayPal and became billionaires.

But not all stories are about wealth or kids who grow up to win Olympic gold medals. Everyone has something to share, and the business world has recognized this. In the *backgrounds. The orchestra, and Gottlieb's work in support of it, demonstrates the legacy of disruptive entrepreneurship, how an innovative project can prosper through the generations and continue to have an impact well beyond the lifetime of its creator.*

I am very aware of the deep power music has—what it can do and how it can affect people. Music is a type of storytelling, and it can stir a rich emotional response. My organization is the fund-raising arm of the Israel Philharmonic, and we have learned that there is so much goodwill that can be built around an orchestra. The work we do plays an enormous role in creating relationships and melting away cultural misconceptions. I feel fortunate to continue the groundbreaking mission of the orchestra's founder, violinist Bronislaw Huberman, who died in 1947, one year before the establishment of the state of Israel.

Huberman created the philharmonic during the onset of Nazism as a way to save Jews' lives. He persuaded top musicians from major European orchestras to migrate to the state of Palestine. He said, "Come and be part of this." His humanitarian philosophy gave the ensemble a distinctive spirit—a spirit we continue with our current group of musicians. Having representatives of Islam, Christianity, and Judaism play music in harmony brings, we hope, a corresponding harmony to other parts of our lives.

past decade, we've seen a surfeit of products labeled "organic," "fair trade," and "cruelty free" finding pride of place in our highly competitive, capitalistic marketplace. These labels aim to connect the buyer to the maker by evoking powerful narratives. Great examples of this type of manufacturing abound, from food to fabric. Peet's Coffee & Tea—whose use of storytelling underpins its tagline "Deep History. Rich Flavor"—works collaboratively with coffee growers around the world. Peet's has helped build schools in Papua New Guinea, for example, and partnered with a cooperative of women farmers in Nicaragua. And clothing manufacturer Icebreaker sources fabrics from merino sheep farmers in the Southern Alps of New Zealand who operate using cruelty-free animal care.

At Lulan, we've seen firsthand the transformative power of narrative. The stories of the artisans and the creation of the fabrics we sell—the natural intertwining of life and work that makes the people and the products unique—shapes every aspect of who we are and what we do. And we seek to share these stories about process, people, and place in as many ways as possible: on our Web site, in our other marketing materials, and on the hangtags on our products. This connects our customers with talented craftspeople throughout the world. "A good story has a way of reaching you at a very visceral and cellular level," Andreas says. "And in that commonality

The orchestra is diverse yet inclusive. Everyone has an equal voice, and we are creating something that is bigger than all of us. When the musicians begin to play, an energy in the room washes over the audience, and you begin to see people smiling from ear to ear. Christians, Arabs, and Jews, who exist in conflict in the wider culture, realize through the process of hearing and making music that they have more things in common than not. In this way, the orchestra becomes an agent for social change.

For adults who are used to hearing their own type of music, listening to another culture's music doesn't always come easily. Children, however, are much more open and respond to music intuitively. With a goal of reaching children in poverty, we're preparing to broaden the foundation's mission by launching a music school and three wind orchestras modeled on El Sistema, the Venezuelan music program aimed at providing young people with alternatives to drug abuse and crime. After learning music, the children, if interested, can join one of the orchestras. El Sistema has been revolutionary for community change in Venezuela, and we hope to have a similar impact here. Music is a universal language, and it possesses healing and soothing powers. In some ways, performing music is like throwing a ball for another person to catch. Music enables us to throw the ball in ways that can't be duplicated. And when the other person catches that ball, it is a very, very special moment.

of experience, stories create a tribe, a community. That's when stories are the most powerful."

Lulan's story-based business model has deep roots in the quest for a sustainable future for the earth and its people—a future we believe our customers want to be part of creating. But sustainability can sometimes seem like an abstraction, and stories give the components of sustainability a vital, energetic reality. When you buy a scarf from Lulan, you buy a piece of wearable art handwoven by a Laotian who is preserving and adapting an ancestral craft while helping support a family. Numbers may be the language of business, but facts and figures alone can be deadening. A well-told story makes a woven fabric come to life. "Buyers understand that the individual or community is going through a transformation and want to be a positive part of that," explains Nancy Duarte, a visual presentation expert and the author of the book *Resonate: Present Visual Stories that Transform Audiences.* "We see the creator's life, journey, and culture, and we have an appreciation and reverence for it. So, we want to help these people improve their lives and work with them to better the situations they're in."

Each weaving cooperative that signs on with Lulan has its own stories, which become, in essence, part of the Lulan story. As our narrative grows, it touches every subject imaginable, from history and geopolitics to culture and personal relationships. In Cambodia, for instance, stories abound about the Khmer Empire when it was at its most powerful, during the construction of Angkor Wat. Visitors today can still see images of *apsaras*, or female figures, dancing in bas-relief throughout the temple complex. Although the stone is worn, it's evident that some of the dancers wear sarongs that are woven in techniques and bearing patterns that survive to this day—and which some of the Lulan partner cooperatives use as well, for both local and international markets.

In Isaan, the northeast region of Thailand, the skilled weavers have a variety of ethnic backgrounds. Small villages in this one region produce many unique types of silk and cotton textiles—including variations of ikat also found in Laos, Cambodia, and India. The boundaries of these countries have shifted throughout history, being drawn and redrawn through conflicts, wars, and peace agreements. The story here becomes not just about gorgeous weavings, incredible talents, and strong cultural traditions, but also about migration—the movement of minority groups and tribes over the course of many years and the ancestral craft they carried with them.

Given the powerful impact of Lulan's rich narrative, we're expanding the ways in which we tell these stories, including giving the artisans point-and-shoot digital cameras and Flip and Kodak video recorders. This allows them to tell their own stories and document their own experiences through words and images. Sonira, at a workshop in Cambodia, shot footage of dyers preparing to add color to skeins of silk. A weaver named Meung videotaped the ikat process, which involves wrapping silk in discrete areas to resist color when the silk is submerged in the dye bath. The weaving cooperatives of Southeast Asia have a rhythm, which is heard in the hypnotic clack and whirr of the loom and seen in the patterns of the cloth. By capturing this rhythm in digital form and presenting it on our Web site, we bring this culture to life and give buyers a more direct link to the artisans and their communities.

People love to see others succeed. If the stories of the weavers—their heritage, their opportunity for economic stability, and the preservation of their craft—can be told well, our buyers will have a different level of commitment to the Lulan enterprise. "Ultimately, customers are not thinking of just buying a product," says Andreas. "They're thinking that they want to be part of something bigger."

With the numerous, swift changes happening across the globe—in climate, technology, geopolitical relationships, economics, and business—many of us distrust the outmoded structures of our world because they no longer reflect real experience. People are hungry for new narratives that represent the movement to make our world a better place, and some of these come from disruptive entrepreneurs worldwide. Nicholas Kristof writes about these kinds of innovators in his columns in the *New York Times* and in the book *Half the Sky*. These new stories are essential because they give us a vocabulary for change and help us see that change coming into focus.

Today, people want a deeper and broader understanding of where materials are sourced and how products are made. Someday, an entire generation will grow up with sustainable products and services. The stories of that generation will need to evolve again to reflect a newer world as it unfolds. But we're in a time right now when stories—telling and hearing them—are more critical than ever. We need strong narratives to help draw people together as a collective to make a difference.

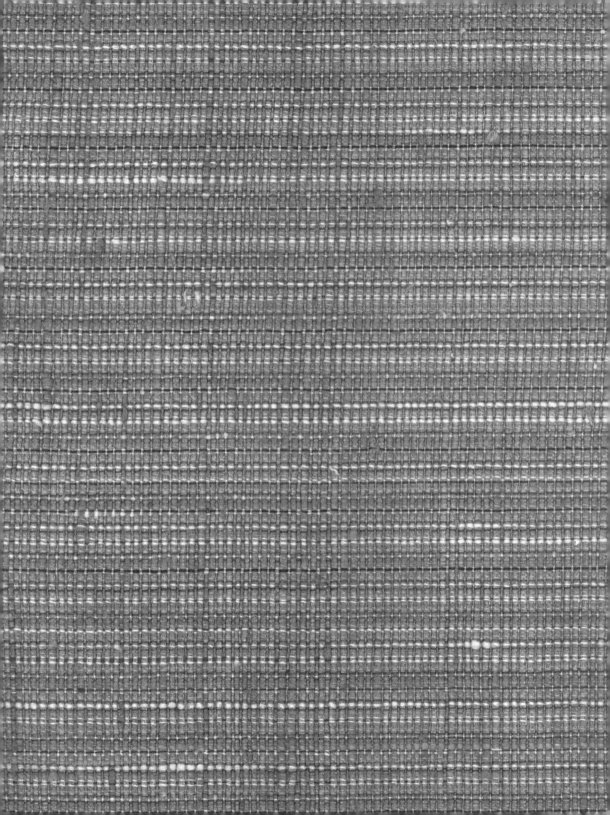

DECENTRALIZE AS YOU LOCALIZE

A CHANCE MEETING

In 2009, I was in Copenhagen at the annual INDEX: design conference. I had just delivered a presentation about Lulan Artisans and was at a party. A woman approached me. Alice had significant experience training and working with artisans in Asia, and she wanted to know how she could get involved with Lulan. I was impressed with her understanding of the weaving process. At the time, Lulan was working in five countries—Cambodia, Laos, Thailand, Vietnam, and India. I told her about my strategy to expand Lulan into other countries through a highly decentralized model in which local community-training centers would act as beachheads to work with multiple cooperatives. We want to expand, but only if that growth can continue to be locally driven, run, and managed.

Alice understood immediately what I wanted to do. She also had the contacts and experience to be of great assistance in finding out if Lulan's expansion could work in Bangladesh. She was willing to do the research—to undertake the "listen" step essential to creating a viable container for collaboration—and to help Lulan determine if we could set up a locally driven operation there. In just a few months, she sent a rigorous assessment about how we could collaborate with groups that had the potential to match Lulan's philosophy and standards of quality. From this chance

HOLISTIC THINKING

In many respects, my architecture training taught me more about designing a business than business school ever did. Tulane University's rigorous architectural program tested students in every way, forcing us to solidly defend every concept we produced. We couldn't simply get swept up in the glory or grandeur of a great design. Every element needed a sound reason to be there.

The nuts and bolts of a successful startup require a similar kind of detailed and holistic thinking. This includes careful planning, clear-headed market insights, and the willpower to punch through the day-to-day challenges of getting your product to market profitably and with integrity.

What I did learn in business school was that it is imperative to understand the intellectual, social, psychological, and cultural nuances of your buyer in order to shape a saleable product. This is true even more so today. Mass-produced goods have the tendency to be just that: what the general public would want. But today's buyer is looking for something that resonates with him personally, something that respects the ecological limits of the planet and has positive social implications. In developing Lulan, I learned that I needed this same nuanced understanding of the artisans—their meeting, a new partnership had developed, and together, we were on the path toward testing this new model of a decentralized branch of the Lulan family.

Lulan receives e-mails from artisans all over the world inviting us to partner with them. Globally, there are millions of artisans—a highly skilled labor force—who are not part of the mainstream economy. A decentralized business model, with satellite branches of the Lulan operation, will allow us to reach more regions successfully. It is important to test in new countries because, for example, local business structures in Bangladesh are complex, which makes it unclear if Lulan would add value to that climate. Collaborations are always key. We know the country has all the right ingredients for our business model, but broader business issues may indicate that the timing is not yet right. It is always best to share openly with potential partners the possible outcomes, whether successes or failures. That is why strong, local, on-the-ground partners are always the biggest reason we succeed.

DISRUPTIVE ENTREPRENEUR
RICARDO TERÁN / AGORA PARTNERSHIPS
Ricardo Terán is cofounder and managing partner of Agora Partnerships, a nonprofit organization dedicated to helping small businesses in Nicaragua and other Central

cultures, religions, and politics. I had to learn their fears and dreams, their hopes for the future and disappointments from the past. A deep knowledge of the maker is important for creating items that fit her, as well as the market.

Lulan resides at a juncture where the wants and aspirations of the buyer intertwine with the skills and aspirations of the creator. Our products have to be attractive and meaningful to both parties. Lulan honors all stakeholders in that we don't simply reduce our clients to being consumers or the artisans to being commodities. Unfortunately, some businesses approach artisanal communities with disregard, assuming that any culture—even one that goes back thousands of years and hundreds of generations—is mutable. These businesses assume, falsely, that outside values, no matter how foreign or insensitive, can simply be grafted onto local practices. This has resulted in the suppression of exquisite cultural expression.

International companies often open factories in Southeast Asia, lured by cheap labor. Promising better wages, these factories pull skilled weavers away from their villages and give them jobs that are noncreative and repetitive. The boiler-room pressure of globalization demands not the craftsmanship of the artisan but the work of a laborer. And when artisans become laborers, they become vulnerable to a fluctuating global

American countries create jobs, protect the environment, and raise people's expectations of what is possible.

When the contra war in Nicaragua started, my family went into exile, fleeing to Miami to restart our lives. There was a very large community of Nicaraguans and other Latin Americans living in Florida for political reasons. I became an entrepreneur at the young age of twelve, when I started my own car wash company. That's when I began learning how to manage and grow a business. For me, being an entrepreneur was something I was born with as well as something I cultivated.

We moved back to Nicaragua after the election in 1993. There was so much poverty, so many health issues, no running water, and no electricity. My father had to restart the family business from scratch because it had been destroyed during the Sandinista years. My father and grandfather felt an enormous personal responsibility. While we needed to build a good company, we could only do so if the people who worked with us were in communities that were more stable. Together, we had to help lift the whole society. That philosophy stayed with me. My first venture was an Internet satellite company in Nicaragua. We sold satellite stations mostly in poor rural areas, and we wound up having a huge social impact on these communities. I became convinced that the best

market. The economic downtown of 2009 hit this region hard. Thousands of young women became unemployed, and this sudden loss of income put them at risk for trafficking. Far from home and without money, many ended up in brothels. The modern factory is an example of an outwardly imposed design system that fails to respect local culture and, as a result, puts workers at unnecessary risk.

The opposite of this method is a holistic, systems approach that first considers people —with a sincere curiosity about who they really are—and then develops solutions from their perspectives. Jacqueline Novogratz, whose bestselling book, *The Blue Sweater: Bridging the Gap between Rich and Poor in an Interconnected World,* describes how she left her career in international banking to focus on philanthropy and financial empowerment in the developing world, considers one of the best examples of intrinsic design to be a solution in the field of drip irrigation, an ancient technique whose use spread in the 1960s after the development of plastic pipe. A farmer brought this method to other low-income farmers in India after taking their needs into consideration. He was thinking of them "as customers and not charity recipients," Novogratz says. "So he looked at three characteristics: One, understanding that the farmers would only risk a quarter of their asset base, which is an acre, so he had to make it work in as little as a quarter-acre. Two, it had to be so extremely affordable that they could borrow way for me to make a lasting contribution was to find ways, through private enterprise, to hire people to grow companies that had strong, effective missions, such as attacking poverty and creating general prosperity.

The role that the government plays in society in Nicaragua is a large one, not only in everyday life but also in the psyche of the people. You have to listen and learn—about the business problems and also the idiosyncrasies—to find solutions that will work with the barriers that entrepreneurs face here day to day. We launched Agora Partnerships to assist these social entrepreneurs. Our local staff on the ground is absolutely fundamental to our success.

One great example is a young Nicaraguan who studied agriculture in college. He felt that he could bring premium produce to the market. He created a network of about 120 women suppliers in a very poor region of Nicaragua's mountains and invested time training them in more sustainable and higher quality agricultural practices. No one was doing anything like this here yet. He guaranteed that he would buy a certain percentage of produc from them. He then sold the produce to restaurants and hotels. We assisted with h business plan and initial operations, and helped him find customers and financir Four years later, he has grown his company into a million-dollar business with fo

money for it and see their investment repaid within a single harvest. Three, the far r had to see that the profits he made from that first harvest could be used to buy a sec d system for the second quarter-acre, and so on. And now, more than 400,000 far rs have benefited from drip irrigation, seeing their yields double and sometimes t le. What we saw was intrinsic design that moved away from commercial-base cust ers to small-holder individuals—low-income people—and really looked at wh hey were as human beings." When we design around the constraints of the proble our solution fits the local culture.

THE CHARRETTE

As we build on this foundational model of systemic design, we learn every da In the past decade, the roles and participation of business stakeholders have truly anged. Our collaborators exist on so many different levels. Buyers, for instance, nov play an important role in product development. Customer suggestions have inspire changes ranging from recyclable bags at Target to beer flavors at New Belgium Brewi g. People can customize T-shirts at Threadless and messenger totes at Rickshaw Ba works, or even fund the development of artists and other projects through online plat rms such as Quirky and Kickstarter. As a result, these companies have avid custom rs who are strong advocates for their products and are active through their online c mmunities.

employees. He just finished building a new factory, which has many environmentally conscious features, including wastewater treatment and solar paneling. These types of companies are invested in the community, and the community is invested in them. They fundamentally believe that the only way to run their business successfully is to play this role. They are not trying to make as much money as possible. Instead, they are part of the community's development, and they know it. This is ingrained in their business models.

As someone who fled and then returned to his country, I can guarantee you that no one would leave his country if it weren't for terrible conditions on the ground, such as violence or political instability that had crippled the economic system. Many people, given the opportunity to return home to a stable political and economic environment after learning some great skills in the United States, are choosing to do it. All of this new, young talent has become a huge source of hope. The more talented people we can attract, the better we will be. Then we can figure out where our society goes from here.

//

To explore this brave new world of creator-buyer interaction, I regularly use a process that I learned in architecture school: the charrette, which is ideally suited to the process of holistic creation. Charrettes, practiced for 200 years in the architecture field, are collaborative sessions in which a group drafts a solution to a design problem. (The term was first used in the early 1800s in France to describe the cart, or *charrette*, used in architecture schools to ferry drawings from hurried students to their instructors.) While the structure of a charrette varies depending on the design problem and the individuals involved, charrettes often take place in multiple sessions in which the group can divide into subgroups. Each small group then presents its work to everyone for further discussion. This process is an effective way to quickly generate a design solution while integrating the aptitudes and interests of various stakeholders. I've used charrettes to design buildings, to design my business—even to design my life. And they can be used at any point in the process to retool all of the above when changes are needed.

Here's how we used the charrette process to create the foundation for Lulan Artisans: Beginning in 1995, I vigorously researched my plan to develop a socially conscious model based on the weaving cooperatives. In the years between the time I conceived of Lulan and when I actually started the company, I had numerous charrettes with designers, weavers, textile designers, and businesspeople. These brainstorming sessions gave me invaluable ideas and support and, in their very fruitfulness, inspired the structure of the company as a container of collaboration. The charrettes galvanized the design direction of Lulan's fabric and the sophistication of the company's overall signature style. They also produced initial advocates for Lulan and helped formulate how to engage a creator-buyer dynamic in line with sustainability. And this process is ongoing, as charrettes continue to shape Lulan and its strategy.

DECENTRALIZE WITHOUT COMPROMISE

Lulan begins with the individual and the community, and the effects ripple outward. Through individuals, we aim to make the weaving cooperatives strong. Once the cooperatives are strong, the artists spend their wages on services in their own villages and towns and in surrounding ones, too. This bolsters their social support network and helps prevent the economic desperation that makes people vulnerable to human trafficking. The artisans gain respect because they bring in money for themselves, their families, and, ultimately, their wider community. Using their specialized skills, they are able to educate and clothe their children. To a much greater degree than they had before, they control their own futures.

For Lulan to expand efficiently throughout many regions and cultures, we need to be flexible, and this requires a highly decentralized business model. Decentralization, as defined in the business world, is the process of dispersing decision-making governance closer to the individuals whom those decisions affect. Decentralization is the "participation of people in making the decisions that matter to them," says Thomas Malone, a professor at the MIT Sloan School of Management. Decentralized business has been proliferating rapidly in the developed world, driven by inexpensive communication—e-mail, instant messaging, and Skype—which has, in turn, allowed a new type of organizational structure to develop. Decentralization brings increased productivity and quality of life for three reasons: it encourages motivation and creativity; it allows many minds to work simultaneously on the same problem; and it accommodates flexibility and individualization. Decentralizing doesn't mean losing control—in fact, it means the opposite. This model can be a quick road to growth while maintaining quality, a design-centric focus, and shared responsibility. Decentralized growth simply involves the addition of nodes to the existing network.

Some businesses are concerned with issues of redundancy and quality control, so they reject decentralized structures and stick with rigid hierarchies. But actually, there's security in redundancy. If your company shares its knowledge DNA with employees, it can delegate throughout the globe with confidence that decision makers will be assertive and decisive. Local training centers function as satellites of your operation and make employees even more independent. With this decentralized knowledge, Lulan can guarantee quality and economies of scale—not only within one country but also in several, when a region has similar skills or techniques. By putting multiple cooperatives to work on the same design, we can microaggregate their work to fulfill large orders. Other times, products cannot be duplicated. A village in Cambodia, for example, cannot match the same shade of red as a village in Laos, because it uses different ingredients. We don't think of this system as fragmented; rather, it is a carefully conceived production process, which allows us to be more responsive to each culture and climate in which we work. This structure encompasses the following vital elements:

Creative motivation

When an industry is in the middle of rapid change, the best way to figure out how to respond is often to let highly creative and motivated people try many experiments. Decentralizing decisions to small groups within the villages or cooperatives, and allowing them to work independently, can often spur innovation.

Diversification

Markets change. So our cooperatives remain strong by diversifying in every way— by clients (from Europe, Asia, Canada, the United States, Australia, and New Zealand), by capacity for production, or by the type of products they make. For instance, if a cooperative is already producing clothing, we advise it to add home furnishings such as pillows or table runners, accessories such as scarves and wallets, and some products for the local market such as sarongs. Conversely, if they're creating home furnishings, we'll suggest they try clothing. In certain countries, weavers can diversify by fiber type. We diversify to reduce risk, because we don't know what's going to happen in the future in terms of economics, politics, natural disasters, supplies, or public taste. Wool may be in demand until a different fiber becomes more popular. A certain fiber's price may increase suddenly, or home-furnishing sales may plunge but later turn around. At Lulan, we offer a wide and changing array of designs, often diversified by product, color, and the markets they are intended to reach. But we always try to focus on classic designs, which we believe have a longer life in the marketplace than trends.

Redundancy

We operate in countries that can be politically unstable. Governments are often in flux. Protests and coups happen regularly. Regardless, we know we can fill orders without disruption, because many of our designs can be produced in different countries. In the last several decades, the traditional business world made a point of optimizing its staffing and production and trimming redundancy to near zero. However, this isn't a resilient strategy. Building in some redundancy gives us more stability.

Customization

At Lulan, we're preserving the traditions and techniques of our artisans, and we are also working with them to expand their knowledge. Our artisans create products in the ways they know best, ensuring that these skills may be passed on to future generations. But when I first met the weavers, I asked myself: Do they have many skills? Do they have varied techniques? Would they be open to making different products for different markets in different regions of the world? Could they fundamentally do that? I believe that through the diversification of skills, Lulan and our partner weaving cooperatives have a stronger business foundation. And this also gives us the ability to be a customized manufacturer.

Design within backstory

No matter how compelling the narrative about a company's social impact, a product won't sell if the customer doesn't like it or think it's worth the price. The quality of the design, color, material, and process must be obvious—almost viscerally so. We are partners taking our products to market, so we have to find a way, together, to position our goods at a price that customers will buy. Only then does it become important for Lulan to share its overall philosophy and the stories of the artisans.

EXPANDING THROUGH "WE'VE"

In 2008, I recognized that Lulan would need new production capabilities and diverse price points to reach and meet the needs of different markets. So I developed a new division of our company, named "We've." Incorporating a hybrid production capacity, We've works with artisans who use electric and hand looms, enabling higher rates of production for larger markets. This side of the company works with cooperatives that have both capabilities—so we can smoothly move back and forth, depending on the size of each order. This structure also allows us to maintain different price points in our two divisions and reach a broader market. With We've, our business can work with a new type of cooperative, which enables us to target a new type of customer interested in an accessible label. In 2011, We've plans to launch a Web site that will sell artisanal goods in a whole new way. This will allow Lulan to directly reach customers and to connect customers and makers more closely through their shared stories.

TO SCALE OR NOT TO SCALE

In any business, a critical question always dominates: What does success look like? Is it composed of one huge win, or is it multiple smaller victories, each important in its own right? Some believe scale is important in design innovation—that unless your business reaches a million customers or ships a million products, you're falling short. Others say that the success of something smaller is purpose enough.

Success is, of course, a matter of definition. Both are right and can have equally transformative results. Great size can be achieved through collaboration, partnerships, microaggregation, and decentralization. But great results can be had on smaller stages, too. Some businesses or products don't scale easily and may, in fact, become less stable and more diluted if grown too large; this does not make their purpose less important. A cluster of small local or regional successes can have the same impact as one large international win.

For instance, the PlayPump had the potential to bring drinking water to thousands by harnessing the power of children at play. As children frolic on a modified merry-go-round, the structure pumps water into a storage tank, to be used as needed. Despite its simple brilliance, the PlayPump eventually failed. One of the main reasons was forced scale. The PlayPump was a great idea that worked locally—within South Africa, where it was developed. Because of this initial success, the pump received a lot of international attention and was forced to scale very rapidly. As a result, PlayPumps were installed inappropriately in areas unable to use or maintain them. This had the unintended consequence of disrupting people's water supply.

Ultimately, the quality of our work within the artisanal and business communities will determine our success, no matter how we measure scale. As Novogratz puts it: "We need to find those men and women who do this wonderful work. They raise all of us, no matter how big or small, to a higher standard."

**IT'S BIGGER THAN
YOU THINK, AND IT'S NOT WHAT YOU THINK**

RESILIENCE, RECOMMITMENT, REVALIDATION

In 2009, on one of my work trips in Asia, I was abducted. Some men grabbed me off the street in the middle of the day and threw me into a car. For more than three and a half hours, I was violently interrogated about my work. From the questions they asked, it was clear to me that these men were human traffickers. They misunderstood who I was and the work I do. They were convinced I was trying to interfere with their business. Human trafficking is a huge industry, and they wanted to make sure that I was not interrupting their steady flow of money, which would easily be in the tens of millions.

The only reason I survived is because they finally believed me when I told them who I am, the work I do, and that I am not in the business of human trafficking intervention. I am in the business of human trafficking prevention using design and textiles to create jobs.

In those chilling hours, I saw, up close, the underbelly of a brutal world. Firsthand, I witnessed women being prepared for brothels and was reminded of how deep, how dark human trafficking is. I knew that this was happening on a large scale throughout the world. And here, I was seeing only one operation in one area of one country. The kidnappers wanted to show me what they do, how this fast, efficient system readies

THE JOURNEY IS THE DESTINATION

When I launched Lulan Artisans, I believed I was starting a company about artisans, design, sustainable fabrics, and the prevention of human trafficking, and that I would spend most of my time working with highly talented weavers and cooperatives doing beautiful work. I anticipated we would assist in social services, such as education, housing, literacy, and health. But I never imagined how much more there would be.

I soon realized that I was not just in the business of fabric, design, and social change. I began to learn about chemistry—how various cooling processes affect the colors of the dyes, and how some dyes are heated and others fermented. I learned that the bark from the linmai flower tree makes a beautiful light green color, while indigo with jackfruit produces a dark green. I realized I also am in the agriculture business. The quality of any regional fabric is dictated by the quality of the yarn that goes into it, and that quality is influenced by the weather in which cotton, silk, and linen are produced. I learned about silkworm farming and the diseases that affect the mulberry trees that feed the worms. I also learned how water is processed and how pH levels are important for the dyeing process. Lessons in land-rights issues and the effects of a fluctuating economy made me wonder how debt affected the ability of these communities to hold onto their own land.

women for prostitution and makes the traffickers rich in the process. They are part of a larger conglomerate that makes up a huge industry. It was overwhelming to witness.

I was in a hot, stuffy room in a dark warehouse. When the interrogation was over, the men walked me out a door into a different section of the building, filled with many small, dingy rooms. As we passed by the first small, damp room, I saw naked girls and women chained to walls, floors, and bed frames. Many were despondent. The oldest seemed to be about thirty; the youngest, barely out of grade school. Some were light skinned; others had darker complexions. This made me suspect that the women were from all over Asia—perhaps Malaysia, Myanmar, Vietnam, Cambodia, China, Laos, Thailand. Some of the girls looked at us, but many didn't even lift their eyes.

This is how the system usually works: men coerce or employ women, often formerly trafficked themselves, to gain the confidence of naive young girls and lure them to places like this. The girls believe real jobs await them, typically as nannies or domestic servants. Other girls are simply kidnapped, abandoned, or sold by their families. When the girls arrive, they often are drugged and then raped, part of their preparation for the brothels where they will service many customers every day.

Why did Lulan get involved in so many different aspects of the system? Because this is how you create a holistic, sustainable business. Everything is interconnected and impacts everything else in the ecosystem—the people, products, and ecology—in many different ways. This is how business should work.

LAND

During the economic boom of 2002 through 2007, land prices around most of the world increased dramatically. Massive foreign investment streamed into some of the developing countries in Southeast Asia to build factories, offices, housing developments, hotels, resorts, and restaurants. People watched their land escalate in value like never before. Investors knew the cities would grow and the land value would increase significantly, so this drove further land speculation, which fueled greater demand for property in outlying urban areas. The powerful and wealthy pressured many local people to sell.

Most farmers and artisan cooperatives own their land. We encourage artisans not to sell and to think instead about the long-term stability of their families, communities, and livelihoods. But while none of Lulan's partners sold their land, many other people did, forsaking ancestral property and then spending the money on items for extended families or mismanaging it, being inexperienced at personal banking. As a result, some

I was led past room after room full of these women. I don't remember how many rooms, how many women. It all became a blur. This awful incident broke my spirit, which I think was the goal of the traffickers in showing me their operation. When they were ready to release me, they threw me in a car, drove me away, and dumped me outside of town. I was in shock, far from myself. I was back in the blank stares of the girls who looked at me. I had seen such despair and need for hope.

I have seen many wrenching events in the last fifteen years of my work. I have heard many stories of personal hardship or plight. But I had never witnessed such a harrowing scene. I think about these women often.

The resilience of the human spirit is amazing. I have met women, men, and children who, even after terrible experiences and ordeals, find an incredible reserve of strength. I have watched them leave or rise above dreadful conditions and go on to be happy and successful. Even in stories of people who are trapped for years or for life, I have heard how they hold onto the hope that one day they will be free again.

Seeing this incredible scene of enslavement up close made me feel an even stronger commitment to my work. Human trafficking is escalating throughout the world. Population

artisan/farmers no longer had land to farm for income and also lost their weaving setups. Many had to start over again, working for others or moving to urban areas to seek employment. This upheaval created enormous economic instability for these individuals and their families. It also proved detrimental to their communities by decreasing the number of residents and therefore diminishing some of the support to keep them strong.

WATER

The ancient city of Angkor is an architectural wonder and a testimony to the power and sophistication of the Khmer Empire. The sprawling complex—a UNESCO World Heritage Site—was the Khmer capital during its 400-year reign in Southeast Asia. What caused the great empire's demise? Recent research puts part of the blame on infrastructure problems and a water shortage. Archaeologists say the people of Angkor cut down forests to expand their farmland. When floods and landslides came, sediment and sand flowed into the city's vast and convoluted web of canals and reservoirs. Fixing the water supply proved impossible for a kingdom already struggling to defend against invading armies, and the Khmer crumbled in 1431. One reason why scientists study Angkor is to learn lessons applicable to today's urban development. With some seventy structures covering about 1,200 square miles (roughly the size of Los Angeles), Angkor was once growth, globalization, international trade, and other factors allow the ease of movement of people and, as a result, fuel this illicit trade. This is an unacceptable practice. Human trafficking impacts all of our lives: it makes us less safe and undermines our communities, our values, and our governing systems.

Many people fall prey to human traffickers when they are in desperate economic situations with no alternatives. Continued research and witness accounts repeatedly confirm that organizations and businesses that focus on generating alternative economic options, providing jobs and creating strong communities, help prevent human trafficking. Through Lulan, I have seen hundreds of people thrive when they have stable jobs, find pride and dignity in their work, and have the ability to support their families.

DISRUPTIVE ENTREPRENEUR
SHASHIN CHOKSHI / AAJ KI KISHORI

Shashin Chokshi is a twenty-year-old student at the University of Chicago. He contacted me seeking advice on his new microlending project in India. I was impressed by his outlook and approach, and we discussed business models, the problems he might encounter, and possible solutions that are relevant to any disruptive entrepreneur.

the world's largest preindustrial city. If a water management issue can undermine an empire like the Khmer, this could certainly happen again in modern times.

Today, the Mekong River is a crucial waterway for many countries in the region. It starts on the Tibetan Plateau in China, forms the border of Myanmar and Laos, turns southwest to Thailand, crosses into Cambodia, and enters Vietnam, where it divides into the Mekong Delta and empties into the South China Sea. All these countries use the Mekong for different reasons, which creates friction over how to manage the water needs of everyone involved. Some people use the Mekong as a source of food for their families. Others fish the river professionally. Still others rely on the river for energy, as corporations and governments build hydropower dams.

Artisan villages and towns use water for cleaning and dyeing fibers in preparation for weaving. Lulan cooperatives collect water runoff during the rainy season and rely on wells and storage tanks during the dry season, from November to May. If the region does not manage its overall water supply correctly, this will impact our ability to sustain our work and keep our artisans employed.

My program is called Aaj ki Kishori (AAK), which is Hindi for "today's young women." It is specifically for young women entrepreneurs in my home country, India. We received a $10,000 grant from Davis Projects for Peace to invest in teaching entrepreneurial skills and to fund microlending projects in India. Over summer break from college, I went home and researched organizations that train women. I ended up working with Seva Academy, a microfinance group that provides basic job training for young women. Many who had gone through this training process wanted to start their own businesses: one in beauty care, another in sewing. We began working closely with them.

I was hoping to help about twenty-five of these women, between the ages of seventeen and twenty-three, become entrepreneurs through an additional two-month training in their focus areas. I soon realized that most of them were creating artisanal goods, such as jewelry, because it allowed them to work from home and have flexible schedules. From the initial pool of twenty-five, I chose to fund two ventures and advise three others. So now I am involved with five startups in India: a beauty parlor, a garment sewing operation, and businesses that produce, respectively, beaded jewelry, bangles, and cooking tiffins.

I faced a number of limitations. Young entrepreneurs have to expand by volume—they have to sell more items—and this was difficult in their small towns. While all were

AGRICULTURE

Some facts:

Supplies of fibers such as silk and cotton in Asia have decreased and prices have increased due to the loss of farmland to urbanization; overall climate change; and a recent surge of natural disasters (floods, draughts, and tsunamis) in the region.

The price of silk cocoons, the raw material for the fabric, has doubled since the start of 2009. The urbanization of Asia's primary silk-producing regions (China, Vietnam, and India) has reduced the amount of land available for mulberry trees, whose leaves are the only thing silkworms eat.

Natural disasters in China, Vietnam, Cambodia, Laos, India, and Thailand diminished the local supplies of silk. Recent climate change–related disasters have wrecked havoc in the leading cotton-producing nations of the United States, China, Pakistan, and India.

Adjusted for inflation, cotton prices are at their highest levels in 140 years; in a recent span of three months, the price increased by more than half. Poor harvests and continued high demand, especially from China, are creating a global shortage.

earning profits in their home markets, the women needed to reach a new, larger client base if they were going to grow their businesses. I didn't know how to help these young women achieve this goal. None of the women had experience in, or even exposure to, marketing, business, customer relations, or design, because these skill sets didn't exist in their communities.

To integrate the markets and expand, we needed to create a network of collaboration among these entrepreneurs. This would involve a phased approach to growth, giving them the power to lead as they became more comfortable with the process. Through relationships and rapport with other entrepreneurs, the women could learn to make their own choices and feel more confident over time because they made those decisions themselves. You don't have to tell them what to do; you just help them through the process of doing it.

A key part of our program is the transfer of technology. But the human connection is still the most important aspect of the relationship, in my own connection with the entrepreneurs and their engagement with each other and potential customers. The hope is that a poor, young entrepreneur becomes self-sufficient by drawing on the knowledge, expertise, and tools she gains from her network.

During the current economic recession, companies have been reluctant to raise prices despite a real increase in material costs. We have been fed a diet of cheap products for so long that price is the driving factor for retailers and, now, buyers. We want cheaper and cheaper products, and this is not sustainable. Climate change and ongoing urbanization are creating a new business climate. If retailers and manufacturers continue to feel pressure to produce low-cost goods, that pressure trickles down to workers, as they are expected to work more for less pay. This puts additional strain on fair-wage employers and opens the door for more exploitation by companies that are not committed to fair-trade practices.

Lulan uses as much locally sourced fiber as possible, and when supply is low, we look to one of the countries next door. Cambodia's and Laos's supplies, for example, are less robust than those of Vietnam, Thailand, and India. We have strong relationships with farmers through our cooperatives and try to purchase from them consistently. Lulan is in the process of deepening connections with farmers in anticipation of needing more partners to meet future demand. We also are thinking of forming joint ventures, in which farming groups would own the land but produce a dedicated supply for Lulan.

I grew up in a city and I work in one now. I've seen poverty my whole life, and it has always affected me. I'm now at the point where I can get involved and do something about what I see. And the more involved you get, the more fuel you seem to have. It's an irreversible trend: once you have that passion, it grows.

Shashin contacted me again when he returned from India. We discussed the specific challenges he faced designing and building relationships in moving the ventures forward. We also talked about the encouraging success he had, launching and advising five startups in only two and a half months. My opportunity to mentor Shashin contributed to his mentoring five other entrepreneurs, and these women will surely mentor others in turn.

IMPACT LOOPS

When you set out on a mission to start a business, you get pulled along with it and grow in ways you could not have foreseen. The social venture movement is not a career path or a business path. It is a life path. My journey, which began so many years ago in the markets of Hanoi, is always evolving. Lulan began as a simple concept and now operates in five countries, working with hundreds of spinners, dyers, and weavers. There are millions of artisans around the world doing work of the highest quality. They deserve to be recognized, celebrated, and given the means to reach new audiences, new buyers. They need economic resilience and strength as individuals and collectively within their communities.

When Lulan works with one artisan, we impact an entire family. Our educational benefit helps children. And the increased wages the artisans bring home filter into their extended families and wider community circles through the products and services they can now afford. We estimate that, on average, six additional people are helped with every artisan in our network. That means that Lulan, through our 650 artisans, has a direct impact on at least 3,900 additional people. And the benefits spill over into the community, too, when the family uses its increased earnings to buy goods and services. We estimate that this indirect impact reaches an additional 20,000 people.

As the world becomes more electronic and transitory—the length of a tweet is the length of a thought—a connection to permanence and the human touch becomes increasingly valued. Handmade products, be they furniture, jewelry, or clothing, help us maintain that connection. The craftspeople who make these objects, who for so long were under-valued, are now being sought out, celebrated, and supported.

To continue our "container of collaboration" model, Lulan created the No Design Gets Left Behind contest, which ultimately allows designers to share their work with artisans around the world. For the competition, we created a design brief for a Lulan collection and invited designers to submit patterns. We posted the open call on crowdSPRING.com, a crowd-sourcing Web site that has 80,000 designers in its community. This was crowd-SPRING's first textile competition and its first design competition using a Creative Commons license, which allows the patterns to be freely used by artisans. In less than three weeks, we received more than 1,600 entries. The competition jurors selected three winners. Lulan paid them for their designs, and, once the new collection is available, we will credit them on our Web site and in our marketing materials.

A panel of leading designers and innovators judged the competition: Ted Boerner, Agnes Bourne, Laura Guido-Clark, Laura Kirar, Michael Koch, Mary Jo Miller, Diane Paparo, Mark Pollack, Cameron Sinclair, and Susan Szenasy. One factor that connects these talented people is their shared belief in the symbiotic role of design and social change. "We know that community engagement can change the way designers think about collaboration," says Sinclair. But "designers have a lot to learn to make this process more efficient and productive. We know how to tell communities how to work with us, but we don't know the other way around. We can go to the grassroots, but our next step must be building a way to have the grassroots come to us."

From sitting in the courtyard of a Japanese house in Middletown, Ohio, to renovating French villas in Hanoi, to working with master artisans across Southeast Asia, my life has brought me new challenges and lessons with every twist and turn. I assumed my schooling in architecture would lead me to a career designing buildings. Instead, it allowed me to design the means to help transform lives—including my own. Lulan has been a wonderful experience. Each day I work with talented artists. I get to know them, learn from them, and see their families and communities grow.

What a gift. Ultimately, I am the lucky one.

LULAN ARTISANS BUSINESS PROCESS

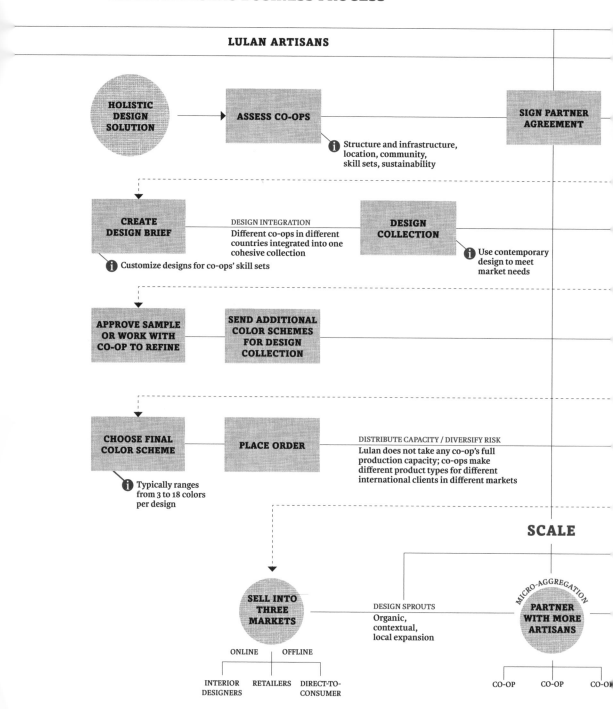

LULAN ARTISANS

HOLISTIC DESIGN SOLUTION → **ASSESS CO-OPS**

ⓘ Structure and infrastructure, location, community, skill sets, sustainability

SIGN PARTNER AGREEMENT

CREATE DESIGN BRIEF

DESIGN INTEGRATION
Different co-ops in different countries integrated into one cohesive collection

DESIGN COLLECTION

ⓘ Use contemporary design to meet market needs

ⓘ Customize designs for co-ops' skill sets

APPROVE SAMPLE OR WORK WITH CO-OP TO REFINE

SEND ADDITIONAL COLOR SCHEMES FOR DESIGN COLLECTION

CHOOSE FINAL COLOR SCHEME

PLACE ORDER

DISTRIBUTE CAPACITY / DIVERSIFY RISK
Lulan does not take any co-op's full production capacity; co-ops make different product types for different international clients in different markets

ⓘ Typically ranges from 3 to 18 colors per design

SCALE

SELL INTO THREE MARKETS

DESIGN SPROUTS
Organic, contextual, local expansion

MICRO-AGGREGATION

PARTNER WITH MORE ARTISANS

ONLINE | OFFLINE

INTERIOR DESIGNERS | RETAILERS | DIRECT-TO-CONSUMER

CO-OP | CO-OP | CO-O

ARTISAN COOPERATIVES

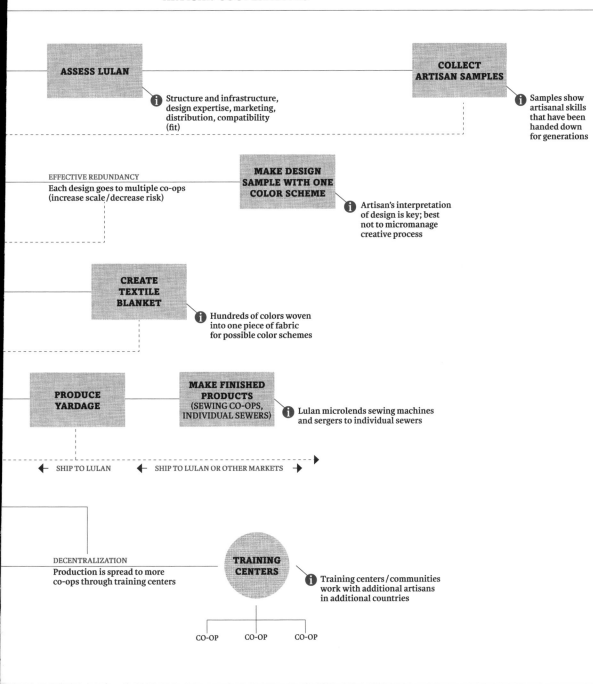

ASSESS LULAN

ⓘ Structure and infrastructure, design expertise, marketing, distribution, compatibility (fit)

COLLECT ARTISAN SAMPLES

ⓘ Samples show artisanal skills that have been handed down for generations

EFFECTIVE REDUNDANCY
Each design goes to multiple co-ops (increase scale / decrease risk)

MAKE DESIGN SAMPLE WITH ONE COLOR SCHEME

ⓘ Artisan's interpretation of design is key; best not to micromanage creative process

CREATE TEXTILE BLANKET

ⓘ Hundreds of colors woven into one piece of fabric for possible color schemes

PRODUCE YARDAGE

MAKE FINISHED PRODUCTS
(SEWING CO-OPS, INDIVIDUAL SEWERS)

ⓘ Lulan microlends sewing machines and sergers to individual sewers

← SHIP TO LULAN   ← SHIP TO LULAN OR OTHER MARKETS →

DECENTRALIZATION
Production is spread to more co-ops through training centers

TRAINING CENTERS

ⓘ Training centers / communities work with additional artisans in additional countries

CO-OP   CO-OP   CO-OP

LULAN ARTISANS BUSINESS STRATEGY

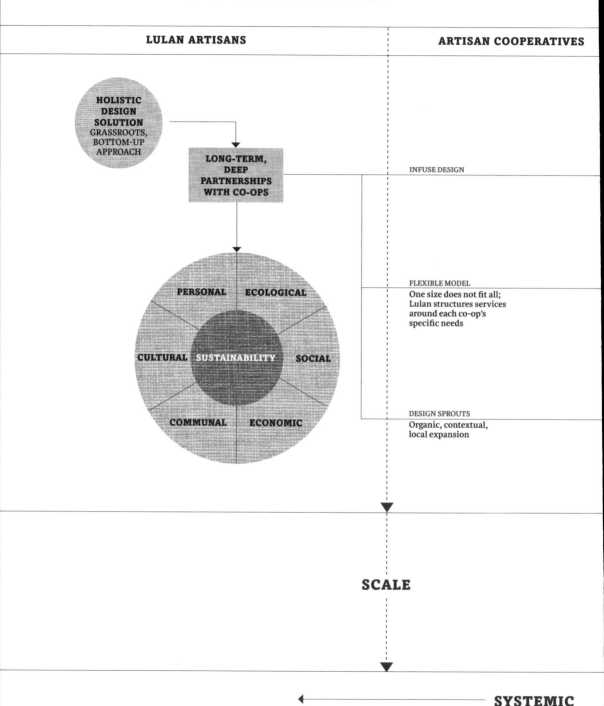

LULAN ARTISANS	ARTISAN COOPERATIVES

HOLISTIC DESIGN SOLUTION
GRASSROOTS, BOTTOM-UP APPROACH

LONG-TERM, DEEP PARTNERSHIPS WITH CO-OPS

PERSONAL   ECOLOGICAL

CULTURAL   **SUSTAINABILITY**   SOCIAL

COMMUNAL   ECONOMIC

INFUSE DESIGN

FLEXIBLE MODEL
One size does not fit all; Lulan structures services around each co-op's specific needs

DESIGN SPROUTS
Organic, contextual, local expansion

SCALE

SYSTEMIC

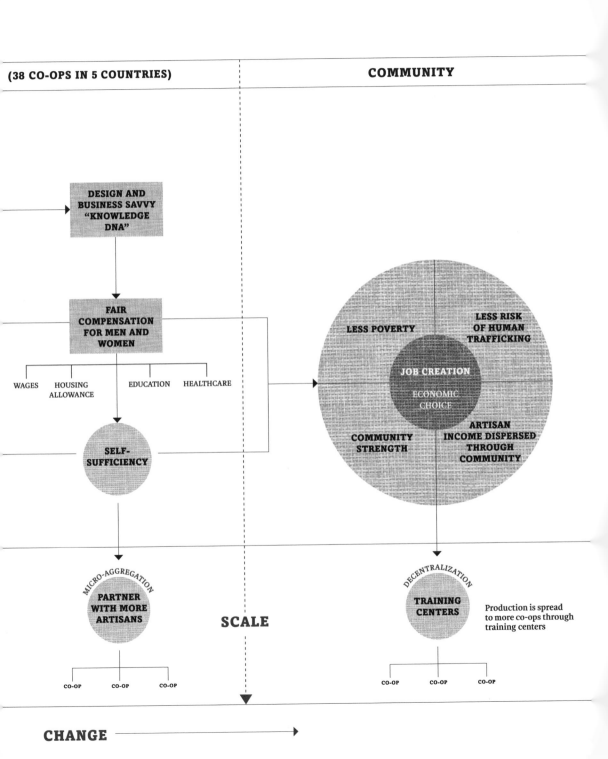

(38 CO-OPS IN 5 COUNTRIES)

COMMUNITY

DESIGN AND BUSINESS SAVVY "KNOWLEDGE DNA"

FAIR COMPENSATION FOR MEN AND WOMEN

WAGES   HOUSING ALLOWANCE   EDUCATION   HEALTHCARE

SELF-SUFFICIENCY

LESS POVERTY

LESS RISK OF HUMAN TRAFFICKING

JOB CREATION

ECONOMIC CHOICE

COMMUNITY STRENGTH

ARTISAN INCOME DISPERSED THROUGH COMMUNITY

MICRO-AGGREGATION

PARTNER WITH MORE ARTISANS

SCALE

DECENTRALIZATION

TRAINING CENTERS

Production is spread to more co-ops through training centers

CO-OP   CO-OP   CO-OP

CO-OP   CO-OP   CO-OP

CHANGE

ACKNOWLEDGMENTS

It takes the ongoing support and care of so many people to help another write a book. In my case, the names would fill page after page. To all of you, I would like to express my profound gratitude.

To the artisans and others I've met along this journey: thank you. Each one of you has made Lulan's work possible. And to the millions of artisans around the world: your creativity enriches all of our lives.

I am deeply grateful for the guidance and expertise of Todd Bradway, Jim Daly, Eric Corey Freed, Horace Havemeyer III, Nathan Shedroff, Susan Szenasy, and Anne Thompson in developing the manuscript. And especially to Diana Murphy, for your ongoing efforts and passion for this project through all of its stages: your energy, support, and experience have been invaluable.

The wonderful photographs of David Costopulos, Mark Standen, Brie Williams, and many, many artisans capture the people, places, processes, and products illustrated on these pages, which were beautifully designed by Paula Scher and her team at Pentagram, Res Eichenberger and Michael Schnepf.

My sincere thanks go to all of the outstanding individuals who have contributed their voices to this book. The dedicated work that they are doing around the world is truly inspiring and transformative, as is that of the thousands of other entrepreneurs and designers who are on the same path.

Lulan is very fortunate to benefit from the ongoing counsel and enthusiasm of its advisory board members: Suzanne Biegel, Allen Blue, Lisa Gansky, Joi Ito, Matt Kursh, DJ Patil, Nathan Shedroff, Cameron Sinclair, Peter Thum, Ann Veneman, and Dale Williams. My humble appreciation goes out as well to Jon Blossom, Laura Guido-Clark, Reid Hoffman, Beth Huntley, Linda Ketner, Michael Koch, and Jim (UJ) Large, kindred spirits who envisioned Lulan Artisans with me in its early days. And thank you to Peter Thiel, Suzan Zoukis, and Stephen Zoukis for your significant support and commitment to Lulan Artisans.

I would like to dedicate this book to Zoe Blossom, now ten years old. Her generation of disruptive entrepreneurs and designers will be able to take this movement in directions that we can't even imagine. But it is immensely exciting to try.

Project director: Diana Murphy
Design and production: Pentagram
Separations and printing: Asia Pacific Offset, Inc., China

Set in Karmina and Amasis MT and printed on IKPP woodfree

Metropolis Books is a joint publishing program of:

D.A.P./Distributed Art Publishers
155 Sixth Avenue, 2nd floor
New York, NY 10013
tel 212 627 1999
fax 212 627 9484
www.artbook.com

and

Metropolis Magazine
61 West 23rd Street, 4th floor
New York, NY 10010
tel 212 627 9977
fax 212 627 9988
www.metropolismag.com

Available through D.A.P./Distributed Art Publishers, Inc., New York
Printed in China

The poem by Fausto Contreras Lazo included on p. 2 is accessible on www.celerina.com.
Sr. Contreras is a weaver with the Natural Dye Weaving Cooperative, Teotitlan del Valle, Oaxaca, Mexico.

Photograph credits
Peter Adams: 20–21; Eve Blossom: 59 top left and right, 75, 106–8, 124, 126, 159; Lulan Artisans: 44–45; RedChopsticks: 8–9; Matthew Scott: 125; Mark Standen: 10–13, 22–23, 43, 57, 58, 59 bottom left and right, 60–63, 70–71, 76–83, 95–97, 113–15, 128; Brie Williams: 127, 129, 141–43